SINK OR SWIM FASTER!

Making a Splash in
Marketing Professional Services

By
Chaz Ross-Munro

Make a big splash! I wish you tremendous success in your A/E/C marketing career!

— Chaz

Sink or Swim Faster! Making a Splash in Marketing Professional Services
Chaz Ross-Munro

Copyright © 2017 by Chaz Ross-Munro

ISBN-10:0-9986801-2-5
ISBN-13:978-0-9986801-2-5

Table of Contents

Acknowledgments

I am grateful for the community of business development and marketing professionals in Atlanta, Georgia and Tampa, Florida that has taught me how to survive and thrive in the professional services industry for the past 10 years. For this book, I interviewed 15 professionals in the Tampa Bay area with a combined total of 250 years of experience. You'll find their inspiration, stories, and suggestions sprinkled throughout the book. A special thanks to Carol Scheafnocker, Debra Costello, Shannon Stein, Anoopa Jaikaran, JR Kozera, Michelle Casale, Ann Schiola, and Tara Krovich for your mentorship, encouragement, insights, and support over my career and more recently as I've started writing this book.

I'd also like to thank Louise Ellrod, Robin Matson, Kathryn Pankow, Ashlee Figg, Mandy Weitknecht, Debra Bauman, and Melanie Jantschek for their insights and fresh perspective on the role of new marketing and business development professionals selling professional services.

Last but not least, I'd like to thank my husband Gregory Ross-Munro, Jennifer Sineway, and Kirstin Pratt for their endless encouragement.

This is for you, Dad.

Foreword

Why should you read Sink or Swim Faster! Making a Splash in Marketing Professional Services? There are changes going on in the architecture, engineering and construction (AEC) industry. These changes are affecting the way we market professional service firms and the people who are responsible for it. Sink or Swim Faster! summarizes the advice of 15 sage AEC marketing and business development professionals to help you and your staff ramp up faster and be more effective!

Baby boomers, many of whom helped shape AEC marketing as a profession, are retiring, requiring new and less experienced staff to take on their responsibilities. The return to the doer-seller model is gaining traction, putting technical people in a very different role with a potentially unfamiliar skill set. And, firm ownership is changing hands at record rates due to mergers and acquisitions that are helping firms achieve growth goals, meet changing market demands or fulfill firm succession plans.

For firm principals looking to hire marketing and business development staff, this book can be instrumental in understanding the key elements of the job, the variety traits of a successful candidate, and critical measures of success. Principals and technical staff being asked to take on or lead the marketing role and people new to the AEC industry will find Sink or Swim Faster! to be the "Cliff Notes" version of the array of AEC industry books on the market. It will give you the roadmap to demonstrating real value to the firm within your first year, and possibly even first few months, on the job. Even experienced marketing and business development professionals will find a multitude of gems of tips and tricks, benchmarking data, and a sound refresher of critical marketing and business development principles.

I highly recommend Sink or Swim Faster! It's a quick read that provides the tools, new ideas, and best practices that you can put to use today to make your firm more successful.

Theresa M. Casey, FSMPS, CPSM
Principal, On Target Marketing & Communications, LLC
SMPS Fellow, Subject Matter Expert / SMPS Markendium: The Body of Knowledge, Multi-year SMPS MCA Winner, SMPS Chapter Champion (San Diego and Connecticut)

MARKETING FOR PROFESSIONAL SERVICES IS DIFFERENT

 As competition intensifies, many professionals are discovering the limits of conventional marketing wisdom. They are finding that marketplace concepts and approaches employed by organizations selling toothpaste, cereal, and other tangible products, or even other types of services, aren't readily transferred to professional services. Indeed, marketing such services is different."

Paul Bloom

Building a Service Brand is Different Than Building a Product Brand

I've been to a lot of marketing presentations by various branding firms. At each presentation, a marketing firm gives examples of firms that sell products like Apple and Zappos, "This is how you do it." The marketing firm then goes into how Zappos isn't a shoe company, it's a customer service company. Selling shoes isn't like selling accounting services, no matter how customer-service oriented the accountant is. Even the nicest accountant must tell you when your actions could lead you to getting audited by the federal government. When you're selling a service, you're both a technical expert as well as a trusted advisor. You can't get fined or end up in jail for buying the wrong pair of shoes. A mistake on a client's taxes can mean serious fines.

Door-to-Door Sales and Cold Calls Don't Work When You're Marketing and Selling Professional Services

When you're selling professional services, much of what you're selling is how you do what you do. It's about relationships. Every now and then you'll need to call someone to set up an appointment, but it's only effective if an introduction has been made by someone your prospect knows and trusts. I've worked and consulted for several professional services firms but the old-school mindset still exists. One employer who sold engineering and surveying services told me that I needed to just stop by each local architect's office and see if they had any drawings that we could take a look at. There are several issues with this strategy:

- Most architectural firms have a receptionist. If I show up unannounced and ask to speak to anyone in the office without an appointment, chances are I'll get blocked right there;
- It's rude to show up without an appointment; and
- If a doctor showed up on your doorstep asking you to be their client, how reputable does that doctor look?

When you're selling a professional service, your reputation is critical to your brand. Client referrals, published articles written by key staff, and conference presentations are a few of the many ways for a firm to establish its reputation. Sending a marketing professional out door to door is just a great way to annoy many of the professionals you're trying to work with.

You Can't List Features to Market and Sell Professional Services

Again, in professional services, it's all about the how. How you market your services is just as important as what you do and it's all about crafting a great story and a way you conduct business that you and your employees believe in. If you would have told me in college that 15 years later, I would be writing a book about marketing for professional services firms, I would have laughed at you. In undergrad, I studied film. In graduate school, I studied entrepreneurship. While one subject helped me learn how to tell a great story, the other taught me how to sell an idea. Marketing for professional services is basically those two skills combined. In this book, you'll learn how to tell your company's unique story (or project experience) and how to transfer that story into tools and tactics that help you win future projects. Telling your company's story in a fun and creative way is the key to winning over your clients.

Marketing and Selling Professional Services Is Really about Educating Your Prospects

A Request for Proposal (RFP) response is really just a tool to educate your client on why selecting your firm to complete a project is the best choice. If your marketing team hasn't done the necessary work to be able to communicate how your firm is different, then your marketing team can't really help your firm win new projects. Building the right collateral materials (i.e., resumes, project sheets, project approaches, etc.) with owners and senior management is critical to documenting how your firm is different from your competitors (differentiation is important and we'll talk more about it in chapter 7).

It's Time for a Marketing Department

The division between marketing and operations happens the moment a firm begins on an explosive growth path. When the firm began, the principal could handle most of the functions and grow the business through referrals. Then, the firm gets its first big client. This client has a project that will take several years and will require the firm to take on more staff to meet the additional work.

As time goes on, it becomes clear that the principal and/owner of the firm realizes he or she can no longer single-handedly manage operations and marketing for the firm. At this point, the firm fractures into an operations component and a marketing component. The principal may not be comfortable with marketing. The reason the firm has grown is because the principal is one of the best problem-solvers for the firm. He or she really excels at performing the service that has led to growth. With preconceived notions of what marketing is, the principal thinks this job can be easily outsourced. The common approach is to just find someone who is extroverted, personable, comfortable with cold calls, and capable of creating new business. The idea the principal has is that the marketing and business development team will take care of the sales and marketing efforts and the operations will get the overall job done, "There, problem solved." Unfortunately, it's not that easy. Again, selling a professional service is different than selling a product.

Building Trust

If you're selling architectural, engineering, construction, software engineering, legal, accounting, or health care services, your expertise and ability to grow your firm depends solely on a prospective customer's ability to trust what you're selling. When you're selling a product, you can analyze the differences and pricing relatively easily. When you're selling professional services, clients have to make a decision based on trust.

When a firm shifts from having a principal doing most of the selling to hiring a full-time marketing professional, it's going to take time for that person to grow the business. Many of the seasoned marketing professionals interviewed for this book said it can take between 18 months and three years to get into a new market. Building trust (similarly to personal relationships) takes time, consistency, and patience.

Growing revenue in a professional services firm requires a strategic marketing approach that leverages the trust, experience, and best practices that your firm has established in the past to attract new clients. In a "Harvard Business Review" article by Paul Bloom, Bloom states "Professional service firms can emphasize three attributes or personality features to set themselves apart: 'gray hair' (more experience, specialization, credibility and contacts), more brains (better solutions to problems), and superior procedures." This book will help your firm capitalize on your marketing and business development efforts. You'll learn how to train your staff through a thorough on- boarding process to teach your marketing staff how your firm's experience makes you uniquely qualified to solve your clients' challenges (if you don't have documentation on this, you'll need to create some). In addition, your marketing team will need to meet each team member at your firm to learn how they add value to the firm or solve your client's problems, and the "secret sauce" in the form of processes and procedures that makes your firm a success.

Communicating How Your Firm Does What It Does

The "secret sauce" of how your firm does what it does is wrapped up in your firm's project experience, history, and how it provides services. Yes, the firm may have a website that details some of the services, but the secret sauce is buried in the mind of the founder. The key to building a fantastic marketing program for a professional services firm is teaching your marketing team how your services – and the way you do them – set you apart from the rest of the competition. The 30-Day Jump Start plan will help your marketing professional gain a solid understanding of your firm, your competition, and clients. The strategic plan will help your marketing team communicate the value your firm offers and what other markets they should target.

After you have a strategic plan, your marketing team can develop your proposal materials. These documents (also known as marketing collateral) will help you communicate your value in a more specific format to prospective clients. Once you have documentation on how your firm does what it does, it will be easier to design an even better web and social media strategy that continues to communicate key messages that reinforce your brand.

Marketing Is an Internal and External Function

Although communicating your brand externally is important, how you communicate the value of marketing and customer service within your organization is even more important. It's absolutely natural for a division to happen between marketing and operations, but what isn't okay is for an organization to value operations above customer relations. When operations is prized above the client, the company will fail. If the designer, software engineer, or project manager make the client feel like an idiot every time the client asks a question, no matter how gifted the engineer is, he or she will be finding a new client to work with if the client feels like he or she isn't valued. The best way to make a client feel valued is to make sure each employee feels valued. Communicating key values within an organization and then externalizing these values to clients is the best way to ensure clients receive a consistent experience. How an organization views its internal and external marketing efforts is key to building a firm with a brand that can grow and evolve.

Marketing or Business Development: What's the Difference?

You may be familiar with the following terms: Marketing Coordinator, Marketing Assistant, Marketing Manager, Director of Marketing, and Director of Business Development. You may also be a little unsure of the differences between the roles. Anoopa Jaikaran, a Marketing Director at a Tampa civil engineering firm says, "Business development is outside sales with a salary. Marketing is inside sales with a salary. Sales itself is a commission-based outside position." Her explanation gives you an overview of the categories and below, I've given you a little more detail about each specific role.

Intern/Marketing Assistant
Experience Level: Little to none
Education Level: High school/Associate degree/Still in college
Description: A marketing assistant usually hasn't been in the industry for very long. He or she may have an interest in graphic design or writing. Your first few months in this position will be learning the terminology, the endless acronyms, and a lot of company research to help create project sheets and resumes.

Marketing Coordinator
Experience Level: 1-5 Years
Education Level: Associate degree/College degree
Description: Marketing Coordinators can have various levels of education but usually have been in the industry for at least a year. Often, receptionists or administrative assistants can find their way into Marketing Coordinator positions after learning more about the marketing functions of an organization and wanting to be more involved in that area of the organization. Marketing Coordinators create resumes, project sheets, have the capacity to assemble 80% of the marketing materials needed for an RFP, and do the production elements of an RFP.

Senior Marketing Coordinator
Experience Level: 5-7 Years
Education Level: College degree
Description: Senior Marketing Coordinators may or may not have a Marketing Coordinator or Marketing Assistant helping with preliminary stages of RFP preparation: resume updates, project sheets. At this point in their career, Senior Marketing Coordinators can write most RFP responses by themselves. The Senior Marketing Coordinator may oversee a small budget for events and other proposal or RFP-related expenses.

Director of Marketing/Marketing Manager
Experience Level: 10+ years
Education Level: College degree/Graduate degree/CPSM certification
Description: At this level, the Director of Marketing or Marketing Manager has probably performed every position listed thus far. He or she is comfortable with a variety of software applications (or may be a little rusty), understands proposal management, can handle multiple deadlines, and coordinating with multiple resources. The Director of Marketing can oversee digital marketing efforts as well. He or she may manage the Facebook, Google+, Twitter, and LinkedIn accounts for the firm. In addition, the Director of Marketing may draft and publish articles for the company website, manage email campaigns, and other

marketing projects (i.e., public relations and client surveys) as directed.

Business Development Representative
Experience Level: 1-6 Years
Education Level: Associate degree
Description: In coordination with a firm's senior management team or Marketing Director, the Business Development Representative will network, cold-call, and set appointments. The Business Development Representative will also help introduce key project staff to clients when a real need for services and a budget has been established for a future project. Business Development Representatives are the most successful in their position when they have a clear focus on pursuing projects in one to three specific markets such as: Retail, Healthcare, Municipal, Higher Education, K-12, or Commercial. In larger pursuits, the Business Development Representative will coordinate a strategy with senior staff, the designated project manager, and marketing team.

Director of Business Development
Experience Level: 7-10 years
Education Level: College or Graduate level
Description: Usually a Director of Business Development or a person performing Business Development duties is all about "The thrill of the chase." Typically, this professional has some kind of background in the industry and went to school for it, or he or she came up through the marketing ranks and now does outside sales. The Director of Business Development will network, cold-call, set appointments, and follow deal flow from the start all the way through to the signed contract for the project. The Director of Business Development may also do periodic check-ins with clients during the project to ensure the client is satisfied with the project throughout. The Director of Business Development will also coach and coordinate pursuit strategy with senior management and staff members.

Chief Marketing Officer
Experience Level: 15-20 years
Education Level: Graduate level
Description: The Chief Marketing Officer (CMO) oversees all aspects of marketing and business development. It is helpful if the CMO has a marketing background as well as experience in business development. The CMO works with the CEO and CFO and helps create the strategic direction for the firm. The CMO will have a budget as allocated by the CFO and have appropriate LOA (Limits of Authority) for expenditures. He or she will also oversee marketing and business development, create a

strategic plan, manage the plan, and ensure yearly sales goals are met. The CMO may also train or hire training resources to help educate senior management and key staff on marketing and business development.

What Kind of Marketing Professional Does a Firm Need?

As you can see from the list of seven roles above, the skill sets of marketing professionals can be quite diverse. Below, I've given a firm breakdown based on company size and the type of marketing support typically found. Since revenue per employee can vary so much between different service industries, I've broken the firms down by the number of employees instead.

Small Professional Services Firms (15 Employees or Less)

A small firm with less than 15 employees typically hires a part-time contractor help build out a website or company marketing materials and the owner of the firm may still be doing a lot of the business development and selling for the company. If the firm can afford to hire a marketing firm at this point, it will prove to be beneficial in the firm's growth as the right marketing consultant can help a small firm create a growth strategy and the marketing infrastructure to win more project work.

Growing Small Professional Services Firm (16 - 50 Employees)

If a firm is growing rapidly and is now past 15 employees, it's time to look at hiring a full-time marketing person. A Senior Marketing Coordinator or Marketing Director will create a marketing strategy and communications plan. He or she will be responsible for implementing the plan. When the firm hits 25 employees, it may also be time to hire a business development professional. Since marketing is more of an internal role and business development an external role, it becomes challenging (and ineffective) for the marketing professional to maintain both internal and external roles. Firms that want to prevent marketing staff burnout and keep a steady pipeline should consider hiring two professionals (one to handle marketing and one to handle business development for the firm). Although it's tempting to hire one person to do both (like a Marketing Director or Director of Business Development), it's not the best long-term strategy for growing the firm.

Medium Professional Services Firm (51 - 200 Employees)

At this point, the firm may now have several office locations, specialities, and service offerings. A 50-person firm should have a Marketing Director to oversee the marketing strategy and ensure consistency in brand messaging between the various locations or specialities. A medium-sized professional services firm may have one to two marketing coordinators reporting to the marketing director based on the budget. When a firm reaches this size, it may have senior project managers or project executives taking on some of the business development responsibilities or a business development professional to oversee the development of new markets.

Large Professional Services Firm (200+ Employees)
Large professional services firms usually have multiple offices and depending on the size of the office, a marketing professional or two at each location. There is usually a corporate marketing team, led by the Chief Marketing Officer, that ensures consistent marketing and brand strategy. In addition to managing the company's marketing strategy, the corporate marketing team will oversee vendors that provide additional marketing services, such as: public relations and digital marketing.

Key Terms and Acronyms
Throughout the book, I'll be using the following terms and acronyms.

A/E/C - Architectural, Engineering, and Construction firms or industry.

Agency - Government agencies and city, county, state municipalities.

APMP - Association of Proposal Management Professionals.

Bid - Same as "proposal" or RFP response.

Boilerplate - Standard documentation often used in proposals, or a lot of the same stuff you'll see on your company's website (i.e., company overview, resumes, project sheets, etc.). Marketing collateral.

CIP - Capital Improvement Projects. When government agencies do their budgets for each year, they set aside monies for larger projects.

CRM - Customer Relationship Management.

Institutions - Universities, community colleges, healthcare facilities.

ITN - Invitation to Negotiate.

RFP - Request for Proposal issued by the client, institution, or government agency.

RFQ - Request for Qualifications issued by the client, institution, or government agency.

RSQ - Request for Statement of Qualifications issued by the client, institution, or government agency.

RFI - Request for Information issued by the client, institution, or government agency.

SMPS - Society for Marketing Professional Services.

SUMMARY

In this chapter, you learned:

1. Marketing for professional services is different than product marketing.
2. How to grow a marketing department and the type of marketing roles found in professional services.
3. What type of marketing professionals you need based on company size.
4. The key terminology for marketing professional services.

In the next chapter, we'll talk about the 30-Day Jump Start Plan and how you can use this plan to get started marketing your professional services company.

THE 30-DAY
JUMP START PLAN

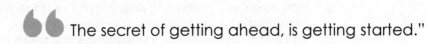

" The secret of getting ahead, is getting started."

Mark Twain

The 30-Day Jump Start Plan

The 30-Day Jump Start Plan is a tool that helps onboard marketing staff quickly. During my first job as a Marketing Coordinator, I quickly learned that I was the only person with a "marketing" title. It didn't seem like anyone really knew what I was supposed to do and I learned based on the requests of my team members. I learned very quickly that I had to "figure it out." This 30-Day Jump Start Plan will help the marketing professional learn more about what kinds of services a firm provides, the staff that provides those services, and research on what makes a firm different from its competitors. This approach to onboarding will help eliminate a lot of the trial and error many marketing professionals experience when first starting out.

What Marketing Is and What Marketing Isn't

Because marketing is an "overhead" or "non-billable" activity, those that may be more junior in performing that function can quickly get roped into other types of tasks that aren't marketing. Requests he or she may hear might sound something like:

> "Hey John, would you mind typing up this spec for me?"

> "Jan, I'm kind of in a bind, would you mind assembling this 100-page inspection report? I've been a little slammed lately."

While these both examples sound like urgent things someone should help with, they'll take your marketing person away from their core job responsibilities and the ability for your firm to win future work. Also, if your marketing person jumps in to help solve this issue, it demonstrates a larger operational issue. It might be time to hire another resource to take care of administrative tasks. If your marketing person is doing double-duty, the senior management staff of your firm may not see an area of concern and you might see this become an overload issue.

What the Plan Consists of

The 30-Day Jump Start Plan starts with one of the biggest and best resources a marketing person for a professional services firm has at his or her disposal: the project team. As Judy Whitaker, a 30-year marketing veteran in the construction industry, says, "The most important thing you can do when you start out with a new company is to learn about all of the people you work with because they'll be your biggest resource when you're trying to solve problems. Plan to get to know as many people as you can and learn what they do. This will help you tremendously. Also, make sure that you have your supervisor let people know who you are and that you'll be reaching out to each of them and getting to know them."

Below is a plan that implements quite a bit of Judy's advice. You can download the 30-Day Jump Start Plan at www.chazrossmunro.com. All of the graphics in this section come from the 30-Day Jump Start Plan.

The best way to use the plan is to print out the checklist; then, the marketing professional and his or her supervisor can discuss it and set deadlines for each action item. Also, both the marketing professional and supervisor should discuss how often they'll meet to discuss each step of the 30-Day Jump Start Plan.

GOALS	WEEK 1							WEEK 2							WEEK 3							WEEK 4							WEEK 5	
	1	2	3	4	5	6	7	8	9	10	11	12	13	14	15	16	17	18	19	20	21	22	23	24	25	26	27	28	29	30
1. Introduction Email (<1 Day)	■																													
2. Website Review (1-3 Days)	■	■	■																											
3. Review Past Marketing Materials (1-3 Days)				■	■	■																								
4. Employee Interviews (1-4 Days)								■	■	■	■																			
5. The Pitch (1 Day)												■																		
6. Finding Professional Marketing Resources (1 Day)															■															
7. Start Creating a Professional Marketing Network (2 Days)																■	■													
8. Meet Existing Clients (2-5 Days)																						■	■	■	■	■				
9. Establish a Differentiator (<1 Day)																								■						
10. Meet and Recap (1 - 3 Days)																													■	■

2.0 - Jump-Start Time line

Step 1 - Introduction Email

An email should be sent out by the supervisor introducing the marketing professional. Depending on how busy the supervisor may be, it's perfectly acceptable for the marketing professional to create the email and then send it to the supervisor to send out. The email should feature a brief introduction about the new employee, an overview of the 30-day plan and how the existing employees can help with the onboarding process of the new marketing person. The most important part of the email is letting all of the employees know that the new marketing person will be reaching out and getting to know each of the firm's employees over the next few days. Below is an example of a possible letter:

Good morning!

I'd like to introduce all of you to Joe Smith. Joe will be our firm's new Director of Business Development.

A Little About Joe Smith
Joe joins our firm with more than 15 years of experience in selling legal services. Joe began his career as a Marketing Coordinator at Legal Serve in 2001 where he stayed until 2007. From 2007 until just last month, Joe was the Director of Business Development for LegalPlus and helped grow the firm from $16.5 million in revenue per year, to more than $30 Million last year.

Joe Smith's 30-Day Jump Start Plan
Joe is ready to help take our firm to the next level! In order to do that, he'll need some help from each of you to help him get on boarded. Over the next few weeks, Joe will complete the following:
* **Website and Marketing Material Review.** Joe will learn more about service offering and will look for ways to help us improve how we communicate our value to prospective clients.
* **A+Legal Team Interviews.** Joe will interview each of you to find out what you do for our firm, and how you contribute to making our clients successful.
* **Client Interviews.** After Joe has a solid understanding of our clients and services, he will reach out to past clients to learn more about why our clients like working with us.
* **Strategic Plan.** After Joe has completed his 30-Day Jump Start Plan, he'll be able to work on a Strategic Plan that will help guide our firm to future growth.

Please help me in making Joe feel welcome!

Welcome aboard Joe!

Thank you,
Marie Chasnoff
President & CEO

2.1 - Email Introduction Example

Step 2 - Website Review

During the website review, the new marketing professional will examine the firm's current website. If the firm doesn't have a website, or it's on the smaller side, the next step would be for the new employee to review competitor websites. As he or she reviews the website(s), here are a couple of questions to make note of:

- What services does your firm provide?
- What market sectors does your firm target?
- Do some competitive analysis. How does your firm compare to other companies that sell your same service?

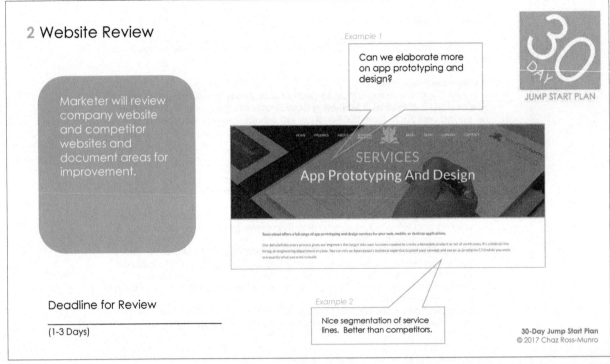

2.2 - Website Review Example from the 30-Day Jump Start Plan

Step 3 - Review RFPs, RFQs, and Marketing Materials

After the website review, the marketer should now take a look at all of the RFPs, RFQs, and other marketing materials the firm has submitted to clients or prospects. These documents are great for helping the marketer understand more about the services the firm offers, how those services are delivered, and key differentiators for the firm.

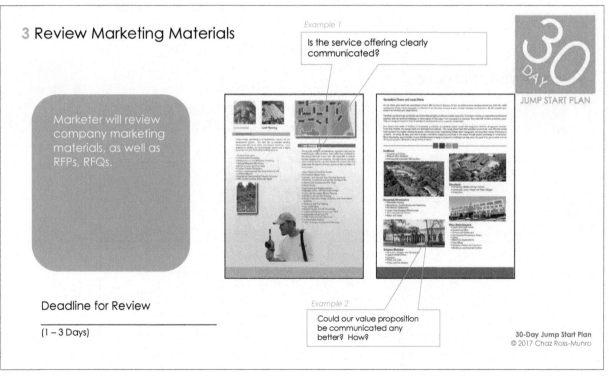

2.3 - RFP, RFQ, and Marketing Material Review Example

Step 4 - Employee Interviews

After a thorough review of the company and competitor's websites, the marketer will begin employee interviews. Questions to ask should include:

- Tell me about your job.
- How do you help our customers?
- What are your favorite projects to work on?
- What types of clients do we typically work with?
- What are our most profitable projects? Why?
- What are our least profitable projects? Why?
- What professional organizations are you a member of? Why?

4 Employee Interviews

Name	Role	Interview Date & Time

Use more sheets as necessary

30 DAY
JUMP START PLAN

30-Day Jump Start Plan
© 2017 Chaz Ross-Munro

2.4 - Employee Interview Planner from 30-Day Jump Start Plan

Step 5 - The Pitch

After a thorough review of the website, marketing materials, and employee interviews, the marketer should be able to describe what his or her company does and who buys the company's services in a 30-second pitch. The marketer should write down this pitch and practice reciting it. The pitch should answer these questions:

- What is your role in the company?
- Who does your company help?
- How does your company help these clients?
- What sets them apart?
- What are some of the biggest and best projects you've done?
- How can someone help you?

5 The Pitch

Example Pitch

Hi my name is Joe Smith and I am the Director of Business Development for ABC Company. My company is a general contractor specializing in the healthcare industry. ABC Company is extremely knowledgeable in medical office building construction and we're well known for refurbishing existing retail spaces into medical office buildings. Some of our most well known projects include:
- the transformation of the XYZ shopping center into the HealthPlus Medical Office Complex; and
- the conversion of 123 shopping center into the HealthisAwesome Medical Office Building.

I'm looking for contacts that do healthcare complex development projects so that I can tell them about the fantastic services we provide. Do you know anyone that I can talk to?

2.5 - Pitch Example

Step 6 - Go to an SMPS meeting and/or Contact SMPS Board Members

The marketer should check out the Society for Marketing Professional Services' (SMPS) website at www.smps.org and find the nearest chapter and then go to the next meeting and find three people to meet for coffee. If there isn't an SMPS meeting in the next 30 days, the marketer should use the website to research the board members and give them a call and ask the questions given in Step 7.

There are fees for an annual SMPS membership, but any professional is welcome to check out meetings and events as a non-member before joining. I have been a member for ten years and I've worked for companies that have helped invest in my career by assisting with the dues. In some cases, I've also paid for the dues myself in order to maintain my membership. When first starting out in the industry, I think SMPS can help any marketer learn new strategies and skills for success. The SMPS professional network alone is immensely powerful.

---

6 Finding Professional Marketing Resources

JUMP START PLAN

Find your nearest Society of Marketing Professional Services (SMPS) Chapter or other industry relevant organization

1. Go to: http://www.smps.org/chapters/
2. Find the chapter nearest to you and go to the next meeting you can.
3. Contact any local SMPS board members and see if they would be open to a phone meeting or a coffee meeting
4. Based on your employee interviews, research additional organizations your team members mentioned. Contact members of these organizations and set up phone or in-person meetings.

Deadline for SMPS

_____

(1 Day)

30-Day Jump Start Plan
© 2017 Chaz Ross-Munro

2.6 - Finding Marketing Resources

Step 7 - Meet SMPS Professionals

Meet for coffee with the three or more people you met at your first SMPS meeting. Ask them these questions:

- How did you get started in this industry?
- What have been your toughest challenges and how have you overcome them?
- Who else would you recommend I talk to?
- What professional organizations do you belong to? Why?

After speaking to a few marketing professionals, you may find someone you really connect with. Ask this person to be your mentor! Work on creating a monthly appointment or phone call that you can connect with this person on a regular basis. Mentorship as a practice benefits both the mentor and the mentee.

---

7 Start Creating a Professional Network

JUMP START PLAN

Start Creating a Professional Network through your contacts at SMPS or other relevant industry organizations

Questions

1. How did you get started in this industry?
2. What have been your toughest challenges and how have you overcome them?
3. Who else would your recommend I speak with?
4. What professional organizations do you belong to? Why?

Deadline for Contacting Board Members

_____

(2 Days)

30-Day Jump Start Plan
© 2017 Chaz Ross-Munro

2.7 Creating a Professional Network from the 30-Day Jump Start Plan

Step 8 - Meet Existing Clients

A great source of information about your company is your existing client base. In this step, you'll get to know your clients (and your new company better) by interviewing a few of your existing clients to find out what your clients like about working with your company. Ask your supervisor if he or she can take you to meet a few of your company's clients. You don't need to talk to a bunch of people, but if you specialize in doing construction for healthcare, higher education, and apartment complexes, you will want to speak to one key client in each of those market sectors.

When you interview existing clients, you'll want to ask them:
1. Why do you like working with our firm?
2. What didn't you like about working with other firms in the past?
3. Is there anything that we can do better?

After you've interviewed a few clients, you'll be able to discover your firm's differentiators in Step 9.

8 Meet Existing Clients

JUMP START PLAN

Name	Company	Interview Date & Time

30-Day Jump Start Plan
© 2017 Chaz Ross-Munro

2.8 Existing Client Meeting Plan

Step 9 - Discover Your Firm's Differentiators Through Existing Client Interviews

After speaking to your clients, you learned why your existing clients enjoy working with your company, what your clients didn't like about working with your competitors in the past, and what your firm can do differently in the future to continue winning over your clients. The next step is to review what you've learned from your client interviews to determine what your company's main differentiators are in your market or industry. Hopefully you have come up with several differentiators, but you want to have at least one.

---

9 **Establish Differentiator**

JUMP START PLAN

Looking over your notes from your client interviews, what were the key differentiators that stood out? How is your firm different from your competitors?

Differentiator

Write down your firm's differentiator in the space below.

Deadline Establishing Differentiator

_____
(<1 Day)

30-Day Jump Start Plan
© 2017 Chaz Ross-Munro

2.9 Creating Differentiators

Step 10 - Meet and Recap

At this point, the marketing professional should feel like he or she has a good sense of the company, staff, resources, clients, as well as a potential network of professionals who can serve as mentors. During the review meeting, topics of conversation should include:

- All of the information gleaned from the website and marketing review;
- Employee, marketing professional, and client interview feedback; and
- Firm differentiators uncovered.

Next, the marketer and supervisor discuss goals for the upcoming year and creating a strategic plan. We'll talk about that more in the next chapter.

---

10 Meet and Recap

Now that you've completed the 30-Day Jump Start, you probably have some ideas about how you want to move forward. Now is a good time to start the Strategic Plan!

Discuss

1. Review of website, marketing materials, and competitor websites.
2. Information gleaned from employee interviews.
3. Professionals contacted and insights gained from interviews.
4. Client interview responses.
5. Firm differentiator.
6. Plan and deadline for creating strategic plan.

Deadline for Meeting and Recap

_____
(1-3 Days)

30-Day Jump Start Plan
© 2017 Chaz Ross-Munro

2.10 30-Day Jump Start Review Meeting

2

SUMMARY

In this chapter, you learned how to get started in your new role as the marketing professional for your firm through a 10-step process that should take about 30 days. The ten steps include:

1. Supervisor Email Introduction;
2. Website Review;
3. Review of Marketing Materials;
4. Employee Interviews;
5. The Pitch;
6. Finding Professional Marketing Resources;
7. Creating a Professional Marketing Network;
8. Meeting Existing Clients;
9. Establishing Differentiators; and
10. Meeting and Review.

Now that you've completed the 30-Day Jump Start Plan, you're ready to move on to strategic planning.

3

PLANNING FOR SUCCESS

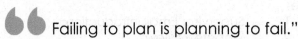

66 Failing to plan is planning to fail."

Alan Lakein

Getting Started with Your Marketing Plan

The words "Marketing Plan" or "Strategic Marketing Plan" can conjure extreme fears of laboring over reports and doing research for hours, but that doesn't have to be your experience. One of the most talented marketing strategists I know, Ann Schiola who is the Director of Marketing for an international civil engineering firm, likes to start off on the right foot with a new company by drafting out a plan while interviewing with the person who will be her direct supervisor: "Over the course of a few hours, I'll be able to identify their communication style, understanding of marketing and how marketing contributes to the firm's success. I've found the marketing plan in itself a great communication tool when beginning a working relationship with senior staff at a new company."

3.0 - Annual Strategic Plan from www.chazrossmunro.com

Once you've done your 30-Day Jump Start Plan, you have a great foundation for drafting your strategic plan. To keep things simple, I've given you a four-step process for completing your plan:

- **Research.** A lot of the information that you gathered during your first 30 days will help form the strategic direction of your research.
  - Did you find out what types of clients your company serves?
  - Do you serve mostly municipalities and schools?
  - Do you work with a lot of retail development firms?

If you don't know the answers to some of these questions, that's okay.

Go back and ask some of your key senior management staff who they typically do work for.

- **SWOT Analysis.** SWOT stands for: Strengths, Weaknesses, Opportunities, and Threats. The SWOT analysis has been a key component of marketing plans for what seems like centuries. In this section, I'll talk more about what a SWOT analysis is.
- **Five-Star Marketing Plan.** I'll go over the key components of your marketing plan. These will include:
  1. Business Development;
  2. Pursuits;
  3. Public Relations and Generating Awareness;
  4. Digital Marketing and Social Media; and
  5. Traditional Marketing.

  By the end of this section, you'll start to see your annual marketing plan take shape.
- **Metrics and Reports.** There is no point in having a plan if you're not going to track your progress. In this section, we'll talk more about being able to track your progress as you work your plan throughout the year.

If you go to www.chazrossmunro.com, you can download an example of a marketing plan, edit the plan, and create one tailored for your firm.

Research

When attempting to solve any particular challenge, knowing as much as you can about the subject and the circumstances surrounding the problem can be very helpful. In your new marketing role, you have been tasked with solving a problem that usually sounds like, "We need to win more work." The next step doesn't usually involve your manager giving you a concise plan on how to do such a thing. After reading this section, you'll have a better idea of how to get started with this challenge by doing a little research. You'll understand the different types of research and how these can help you understand your work challenges and you'll start to see how you can use your research to plan winning strategies for bringing more work to your firm.

Types of Research: Primary and Secondary

"A/E/C Marketing Fundamentals: Your Keys to Success" by Ronald Worth, Holly Bolton, and Julie Huval offers a good summary of types of research in the A/E/C industry. There are two types of research: primary and secondary research.

Primary research is usually research you can conduct yourself through in-person interviews. You started doing this during your initial 30-Day Plan when you interviewed fellow team members in your organization. While you're working on your Annual Plan, you may want to expand on this by interviewing clients either in-person or by phone. Interviewing your firm's clients is a great way to gain additional insights into your organization. Some of the key senior staff in your organization can help you identify good sources for interviews.

Secondary research uses information collected by another party. Good sources of secondary research include trade organization reports and surveys or additional information you find online through internet searches.

Follow the Money
In your first 30 days when you interviewed your team members, you started to figure out what market sectors most of your clients come from. When you start conducting your research, you'll need to focus on some of those areas to determine where most of their funding sources will be coming from in the upcoming year.

Researching the Public Sector: CIP Budgets
A good way to determine which government agencies you should be targeting is by looking at their CIP budget or Capital Improvement Project budget. Every city and county agency has a CIP budget. Your first step in this process should be to determine which agencies have money allocated for the product or service you sell. You can use this information to dictate how much time you spend during the year chasing work with the specific agency.

The good news is that most government agencies have their CIP budgets accessible online. Let's say your company specializes in roofing construction services, the best way to determine if the agency that you're pursuing has the money is by checking out their CIP budget and also their regular budget to see how much money the agency has allocated for construction projects and maintenance. I wish I could tell you sifting through this information is easy, but it can be a little time intensive. If you don't have a lot of time, just focus on the three clients your company has already done work with and pull their budgets to start. We'll get more into the specifics of what to do with that information in the Business Development Chapter. At this point in the plan, you just want to identify possible projects that might fit with the type of project work you do at your firm.

Researching the Private Market Sector

In many ways, the public sector is a little easier to research since a lot of the information is posted online with a purpose of being "public information." It can get a little trickier when you want to do research in the private sector. The best way to research the private sector is to look at specific markets within the sector, for example: Healthcare, Multi-Family, Residential, Retail, and Commercial.

Larger firms are probably concerned with the size of each respective market and this can usually be billions to trillions of dollars. If you're working for a firm that's under 100 people and you are regionally focused, this kind of information may be too high level to be useful. In this case, sticking to the information given in the regional economic development councils with the most relevance to your firm would be the most useful. For example, since I'm in Tampa, Florida, I'm going to do research on four to six counties that are the closest to me, so I'm going to check out the economic development data for Hillsborough, Pinellas, Pasco, Polk, Sarasota, and Manatee counties.

I'm also going to check out a few local professional organizations to see if they have programs coming up or published reports on economic data I can include in my report. When you started your 30-day onboarding plan, you may remember I suggested asking your fellow team members and SMPS members which professional organizations they participated in. As you do more extensive marketing research, the feedback you received will give you a little strategic direction as to where you should be focusing your research.

Day-to-Day Research on Current Events

I do a lot of my research on a day-to-day basis with a social media platform called buffer (www.buffer.com). Since I manage the social media accounts for my company, I like to use the RSS feeds to catch up on industry news and then to share news with connections and followers.

SWOT Analysis

As mentioned earlier, SWOT stands for: Strengths, Weaknesses, Opportunities, and Threats. Strengths and weaknesses pertain to your organization. Opportunities and threats represent external forces that may affect the trajectory of your company during the upcoming year. In the 30-Day Jump Start Plan, you interviewed current and past clients. This information will be useful as you conduct your SWOT analysis. Carol Scheafnocker, a 30-year marketing veteran says, "Be sure to realize internal opinion may be different than external opinion. Do your research and know what clients and former clients think about you. No firm is perfect."

A SWOT analysis is like setting up your firm's GPS. After your completing your 30-day onboarding plan, you probably have an idea of where your firm is trying to go, but you have to know where you're starting. A SWOT analysis helps you determine your starting point in the market. By asking yourself and your company a few questions, you can gauge your current location and what direction your firm needs to take to get to your overall goals for the year or next few years.

Completing a SWOT Analysis is a useful exercise for your marketing plan but it can also be helpful when creating a strategic plan for your proposal pursuit. If your company is pursuing a large project, analyzing your situation by performing a SWOT analysis can help your company develop a solid strategy for securing the project. It can also quickly help you determine if it might be worth you even attempting to pursue the work at all, resulting in a "no-go." (More on no-gos coming in later chapters.) I've given you a template for your SWOT analysis at chazrossmunro. com so after you've read a little more about the analysis, make sure you download it and begin completing it for your marketing plan.

Strengths	Opportunities
Strengths are focused **internally** within the organization. Goal is to increase the amount of strengths your firm has.	Opportunities are focused **externally** within the market your firm serves. Work to increase the amount of opportunities.
Weaknesses	**Threats**
Every organization has their **internal** weaknesses. List them here. The goal is to decrease the amount of weaknesses your firm has.	Threats are focused on those **externally** within the market. Work to decrease the amount of threats.

3.1 SWOT Analysis Template

Strengths

You probably became familiar with some of your organization's strengths when doing your interviews. You may have heard things like, "We're a woman-owned firm," "Our safety program is second to none," and "Our people are the best." All of these components can be considered strengths.

Weaknesses

When you interviewed employees, you probably heard things like, "I wish we had more expertise in senior living," "Our staff is pretty young and we don't have as much depth on our team as some of our competitors do," or "We're a small firm and don't have extensive resources." These phrases are good examples of perceived weaknesses in your organization.

Opportunities

When you were hired, you probably heard things at your interview that will clue you in on what opportunities some of the senior management staff at your firm see in the market, for example, "We would really like someone to help us with our proposals for municipalities. The public sector is starting to have a lot of work available that we're well suited for." Therefore, an opportunity you want to address is growth in the public sector. You also may have discovered some opportunities while performing your market research. Start listing the opportunities for growth that you found in this section of your SWOT analysis.

Threats

Threats pertain to external issues affecting your organization. Is there a new competitor in your area that is starting to do similar work? Is there an economic factor that may affect future opportunities? Possible threats may be things like the port closing down if your firm does a lot of work for a nearby port, labor shortages, and new regulatory issues that may impact your firm's business. Again, you probably uncovered some of these while doing your initial discussions with your team members or from some of your marketing research.

SWOT Analysis Summary

Uncovering your firm's strengths, weaknesses, opportunities, and threats by performing a SWOT analysis is a useful tool for both your marketing plan and proposal pursuits. By spending a little time examining these key components, you'll have a better idea of how to chart your company's success in the future.

Marketing Plan

You've now completed your 30-day Jump Start Plan, primary and secondary research, as well as your SWOT analysis. It's time to put all of your research into a marketing plan. To keep things simple, we're going to focus on five key components and set goals for: Pursuits, Business Development, Public Relations, Digital Marketing, and Traditional Marketing. If you go to chazrossmunro.com, you can download a sample marketing plan in a PowerPoint template.

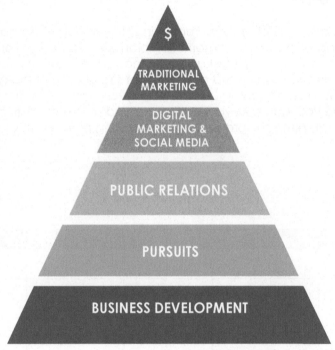

3.2 - Marketing Professional Services Pyramid

If you do a little internet research on "sales funnels," you'll see I've structured my marketing plan in reverse of the sales funnel. I structured it this way because when you're starting out, trying to create a multi-faceted marketing strategy is a little tough until you have a thorough understanding of the consulting services you're selling. The best way to get a grasp on your business and to directly make an impact is to focus on developing business relationships and the materials you'll need to submit a winning proposal.

Use SMART Goals in the Marketing Plan

When you work on the marketing plan, your goal is to create a document that communicates marketing responsibilities and goals for the firm. To set these goals, we'll use SMART goals when possible. SMART is an acronym for:

- Specific
- Measurable
- Achievable
- Relevant, and
- Time-Bound.

Since you may be new to your marketing role, setting these goals may be a little challenging. Your first marketing plan is version 1.0. Throughout the year as you learn more, it's okay if you end up with version 5.6. The point of the marketing plan isn't to get it perfect straight out of the gate. Rather, the point is to clearly communicate your goals and the tactics you'll use to achieve your goals. As you learn more and gain more experience, your ability to complete a more accurate marketing plan will only improve.

Annual Strategic Marketing Plan
© 2017 Chaz Ross-Munro

Public Relations
1 & 2 Professional Organization Participation Goals

No.	Organization	Targeted Market Sectors	Attendees	Goal for Attendance	Budget	Participants

3.3 - SMART goals template for public relations component of strategic marketing plan

Create a Revenue Goal

Based on your research, you may have discovered an industry growth projection for the year; you can use that as the growth goal for your firm's revenue projection. For example, if your research determined a 7.4% growth rate in the construction industry for the next year, use that number. So, if your firm achieved $1 million in revenue last year, you would set your goal at $1,074,000 for this year ($1,000,000 x .074 = $1,074,000). The rest of the components of your marketing plan will help you create tactics to reach that revenue goal. If you're looking for a way to project how many proposals you'll need to complete in order to achieve that revenue goal, just use the number you have for this year and multiply it by 7.4% growth, round up, and that should give you a good target for this year.

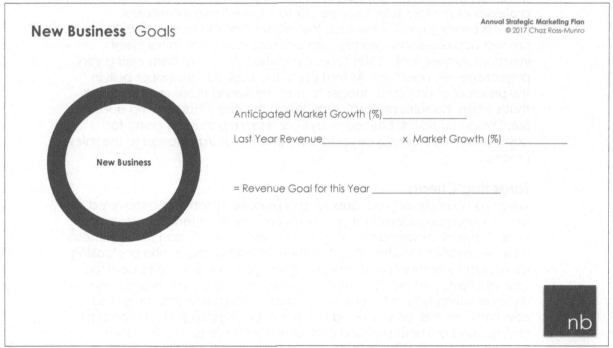

New Business Goals

Annual Strategic Marketing Plan
© 2017 Chaz Ross-Munro

New Business

Anticipated Market Growth (%)_____

Last Year Revenue_____ x Market Growth (%) _____

= Revenue Goal for this Year _____

nb

3.4 - New Business Goal Worksheet

Business Development - Connecting with and Qualifying Clients

When you're first starting out in your role with a professional services firm, you may not be directly responsible for business development. However, chances are you'll start to get involved with some of these activities as you grow in your marketing role. The business development components of your plan will include:

A.   Targeting Clients;
B.   Professional Organizations;
C.   Conferences;
E.   Lead Generation; and
G.   Prospect Meetings.

Business Development Is Not Sales

Business development and sales can sometimes get mixed up, so I thought I'd spend a little time going over the differences. Business development occurs very early in the sales process. Most deals in professional services take between six to 18 months to materialize. Business development is the face the client begins to see early in the process at professional organizations, conferences, and initial client introductory meetings. Sales takes over when the client starts asking very project-specific questions. At that point, the business developer pulls in the principal or project manager to start answering those questions and that's when the sales process starts. When the client starts asking questions like, "When could I get this done by?" or "How much is this going to cost?", then the business development phase has transitioned to the sales process.

Targeting Clients

When you completed your onboarding plan, you probably discovered a few of the organizations that your firm's employees attend on a regular basis. Some of these may be to grow their own careers and some of these may be organizations that help put them in front of those who are looking for your firm's products and services. When you spoke to staff about the type of clients and projects they're working on, it probably helped you discover which types of clients you should be targeting. Hopefully, you now know the person you need to talk to about getting a list of the past clients. Find out who the most profitable clients were, and look for ways to connect with clients similar to the most profitable ones.

Client Mix

When targeting clients, a lot of professional services firms create a mix of both public and private sector targets. This is a long-term strategy that pays off during economic downturns. During the Great Recession from 2007 to 2009, a lot of firms in the construction industry were put out of business if they only focused on private sector work. The companies that survived had both public and private sector work. Public sector work is a great way to shore up your client base for the long term. When the private sector is struggling, public sector work - perhaps not always the most profitable - can keep your business afloat and the doors open.

Whether times are good or bad, if you choose to make public sector work part of your overall marketing plan, make sure you are consistent in your marketing and business development efforts. Your process should begin with a thorough review of the Capital Improvement Project (CIP) budgets for each respective municipality you're planning on targeting. CIP budgets are incredibly useful in determining which public organizations have money allocated for the type of service your company provides. If you take the time to review CIP budgets, you'll be able to spend a lot of time chasing clients that have enough money for your product or service. If not, you can spend a lot of time on companies that can't afford you.

Professional Organizations and Conferences

One of the best ways to connect with clients is at professional organizations. If I want to connect with facilities managers for major healthcare organizations in Florida, then I'm going to go to the Agency Healthcare Administration (AHCA) and Florida Healthcare Engineering Association (FHEA) meeting in Orlando each year. At this conference, I can hear lectures about the topics my clients might be interested in, and will have the opportunity to network with them. During this phase of the process, my job isn't to try and sell them anything. My job is to get to know the key players, what kinds of things keep them up at night, and start to brainstorm services my company has that might be able to help them. Based on what professional organizations and conferences you target, you may need to set up appropriate budgets.

Another important way to connect with possible clients is to become members or serve on the board of directors for important professional organizations in your industry. For example, if you are a board member for the Programs Committee and responsible for creating monthly events, it will also be your responsibility to find speakers. The speakers you will need to contact will usually be high-profile representatives at target organizations. This is another great way to get in front of prospects and give you an ideal opportunity to follow up with key prospects about future projects.

Prospect Meetings

After completing your CIP research, attending some professional organization meetings, and doing some general cold-calling, you may have a list of people that you've targeted for meetings. The primary goal in setting up meetings is to discover when a project might be ready for you to bid. It's a good idea to have a plan for each pursuit on how many times you'd like to meet with a client before the RFQ or RFP comes out.

Lead Generation

If you are chasing public or institutional clients, chances are you'll hear about an upcoming RFQ or RFP from department heads at that organization before an RFQ or RFP is released. You may have heard of Demandstar, Onvia, IMS, BidSync, or a few other bid services that provide you an emailed list of RFQs and RFPs that have been released each day. It doesn't really matter which service you use for lead generation, it just matters that you have a process for discovering which opportunities are coming, and then a way to find the RFQ or RFP when it's released.

Business Development Goal Setting

If business development falls under your job description, then you'll want to set some goals.

Item	2017	Budget	2018 Goals
Organizations Targeted	REIC TBBA NAIOP SMPS	$475 $200 $300 $400	1 meeting quarterly 1 meeting each month 1 meeting quarterly 1 meeting each month
Conferences Attended	AHCA FEFPA	$2,000 $2,000	Attend Annual Conference
Prospect Meetings	500	$50 per lunch $200 per dinner	50 each month or 600 for the year
Pursuit Win Rate	50%	$2000 each	Increase pursuit win rate to 75%

3.5 Business Development Goal Matrix

Pursuits

This section of your plan will help you identify how you'll qualify opportunities with your senior management team and/or supervisor, what kinds of proposal materials you'll need to build to support your proposal efforts, how many opportunities you'll need to pursue, and how many presentations you'll need to make. First, I'm going to elaborate on what each item is and then we'll work through what your goal needs to be for each one.

- **General Qualifications Packages** - Qualifications packages for a professional services firm typically consist of a company overview, company experience, bios or resumes of key staff, and a list of the services your firm offers.

- **Prequalification Packages** - Prequalification packages can vary depending on the client (public or private sector). If you are submitting a prequalification package for a public entity or municipality, these can be quite extensive, requiring tax information and/or financials. Sometimes, it may be as simple as submitting information that is on a W-9 form.

- **Request for Qualifications** - A Request for Qualifications or RFQ is a document issued by an organization that explains what types of products or services it's interested in buying. If the service requested in the RFQ is a specialty of your firm, then you may choose to submit your qualifications. Usually an RFQ is several pages long and specifies exactly what the firm is looking for. It is your job to submit all necessary requirements and to prove (in writing) how your firm is the best firm to provide these services. An RFQ is usually "qualifications-based," which means price is a factor, but it is more important that you demonstrate your firm is qualified to do the work, then price negotiation will usually come a little later in the process.

- **Request for Proposals** - A Request for Proposal (RFP) is very similar to an RFQ, except price now becomes a larger factor in the overall selection. Not only does the organization issuing the RFP want to see if you're qualified to handle the work, it also wants to know if your pricing is competitive as well.

- **Shortlist Presentations** - A shortlist presentation usually occurs after your firm has responded to an RFQ or RFP and the organization has determined that your firm meets all necessary requirements and is qualified to provide the service required. The organization now wants to meet your firm in a face-to-face meeting and get to know you a little better, similar to an interview after applying for a job. Since providing a service takes time and usually results in you working closely with the organization, the selection committee is now trying to determine if they'll like working with your organization. At this point, the process gets more subjective.

Creating Goals for Pursuits

If your organization submitted RFQs, RFPs, and did some presentations last year, you're in luck. Just take those numbers, add your growth percentage (we used 7.4% above) and you're done. Like this:

Item	2017	Growth	2018 Goals
General Qualifications Packages	48	48*.074 = 3.55	48+4 = 52
Pre-Qualifications	12	12*.074 = .88	12+1 = 13
RFQs / RFPs	24	24*.074 = 1.776	24+2 = 26
Presentations	6	6*.074 = .444	6+.44 = 7

3.6 Pursuit Goal Matrix

Since this is your first year out, projecting your goals this way is a good start. However, as you continue to grow in your role, you may start to realize that you are submitting a lot of responses to RFQs and RFPs but you're not winning a lot of them. If this starts to happen, you definitely want to cut the quantity of submittals. This means, you'll have to do a better job of qualifying clients and pursuits.

Public Relations and Generating Awareness

You may need to address public relations efforts in your marketing plan, which in addition to joining professional organizations and boards, can include items like submitting press releases and community outreach (we'll also go more into more detail on public relations and generating awareness in Chapter 12).

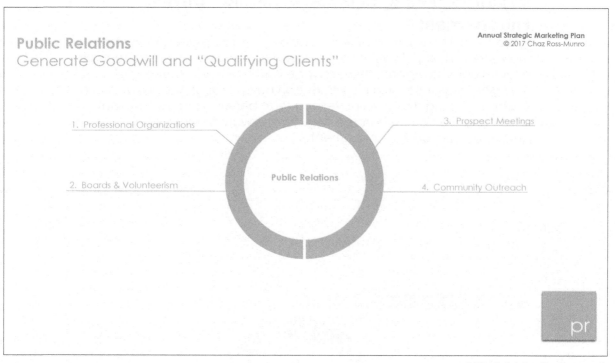

3.7 Public Relations Plan Components

Press Releases

Depending on your budget, you may have a public relations firm that supports your business. Most companies I've worked with between 10-25 people, typically don't have the budget to work with a PR firm and use free sources to submit press releases. Press releases for a professional services firm include things like: new employee hires, new project wins, projects completed, and speaking engagements. You want to do a press release at least quarterly and make sure they are placed on your company's website.

Community Outreach

Depending on what your organization does, finding some ways to engage with nonprofits may be a good way to build morale and get some positive recognition for your firm. If you work for a software engineering company, volunteering your staff to help kids learn how to code for an afternoon is a great way to generate some positive buzz about your organization in the community. Community outreach offers another great opportunity for building your public relations presence.

Digital Marketing and Social Media - Driving Engagement

Depending on what market you're serving, your approach to digital marketing will vary. If you're working for a civil engineering, architect, or general contracting firm, there may be a little misunderstanding about the benefits digital marketing efforts can have for your company. Most digital marketing strategies have long-term benefits despite needing a day-to-day effort to manage. You always want to make sure you're getting a return on your investment.

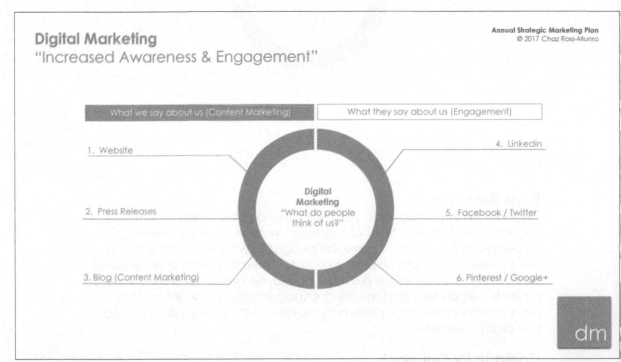

3.8 - Digital Marketing Plan Components

Digital marketing involves setting goals for each of the following:

- Company website;
- Company blog;
- LinkedIn;
- Facebook;
- Twitter;
- Google+; and
- Pinterest.

Goals for digital marketing during your first year, may be just to create a regular blogging schedule. Since this is your first year, start with something you can definitely achieve and this might only be one blog post per month. That's okay. Starting the practice of blogging can be extremely beneficial. If your company's website hasn't been updated in a few years, chances are that might be something you get roped into right away. If you were hired specifically to redo the website, then that's something you should tackle right away. However, if you're new to the industry, I would recommend waiting at least six months to a year before redoing the website. If you don't have a good grasp of what your company does and why it does it, it's going to be a challenge to design a website that really excels at promoting your firm. Also, if you hire a consulting partner to help with the website design, the consulting firm will have a hard time helping you if you don't have a thorough understanding of your company. We'll talk more about digital marketing tools in Chapter 11.

Traditional Marketing Goals

Traditional marketing involves all the tangible stuff you think of when it comes to marketing. Items that fall under this category include:

- Signage on company equipment or cars;
- Signage on project sites;
- Business cards;
- Brochures;
- Handouts;
- Advertising;
- Employee shirts/hats;
- Company swag (i.e., branded keychains, USB drives, golf balls, etc.); and
- Client appreciation gifts.

When you begin laying out your plan for traditional marketing, you want to identify who will handle ordering and budgets for the items involved. It can be that simple for this component of the plan. For your first draft of the plan, you may not have all of this information so you'll need to communicate with your supervisor to obtain any missing details.

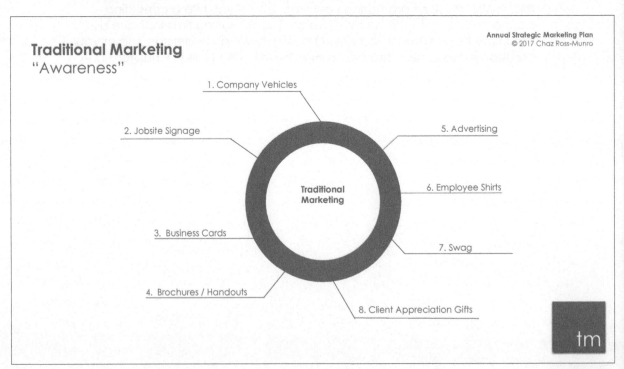

3.9 - Marketing Plan Components

Metrics and Reporting

As you work on your marketing plan, talk to your boss about establishing metrics and reporting. Your boss, or a lot of the principals at the firm, may have grown their business by referrals and may not really understand the value a marketing professional will bring to a firm. How you go about marketing the firm and/or selling the firm will be a little different than how your senior staff sells their services. It will be helpful for you to establish goals and metrics so you have a good way to gauge your progress throughout the year.

Creating a way to measure your success throughout the year is a great way to maintain motivation. If you've ever tried to lose a few pounds, the real success happens when you start logging what you eat and paying attention to whether or not you remain under your calorie goal for the day. Without tracking your diet, it's really hard to lose weight and meet your goals. The same philosophy you use for setting goals with your health and fitness regimen can be applied to your marketing goals. If you can keep track of your proposals, contacts, and other marketing activities, you'll be able to determine if you're on track to meet your goals.

Generational Differences and Expectations

Based on the type of firm you work in, company culture, and maybe even the age of your supervisor, he or she may have different expectations than you when it comes to reporting in and the metrics they'll use to judge the success of your job. For most of my career in the engineering and construction industry, I worked with a lot of "Baby Boomers" or those born between 1946 and 1964. Generally, my supervisors didn't require a lot of input from perceived subordinates. My paycheck was my signal that I was doing a good job and that I was appreciated. These supervisors were pleased if I checked in with them once a week or every other week. Communication in person or by phone was preferable.

When I began consulting, I started working with Generation X (born 1965-1979) and these professionals seem to be perfectly okay working alone or in small groups. Email communication was preferable and they rarely required face-to-face interaction.

The tech-savvy Millennials (born 1980-2000), seemed to appreciate a Twitter-like communication feed through text, Skype, or email. Daily mini-updates seemed to keep the Millennials happy as opposed to long email correspondence.

Although I mentioned the different approaches and communication styles above, these are just generalities. You'll still want to make sure your supervisor is clear on how you'll be checking in, the amount of times you'll be checking in, and how you'll communicate your goals.

Daily Goals for the First 30 Days

When you first start out at a firm, you may need to establish daily goals with your supervisor. You will want to check in each day, talk about what you plan on working on, contacts you plan to make, and get your supervisor's feedback. When you leave for the day, check in with your supervisor to let them know what you've been working on. Each time you meet, it should only be 10-15 minutes. The idea isn't to have a long meeting where you explain the minutia of everything you've done. This meeting will help you understand how long some of the components of your job actually take so you can accurately set longer-term goals. You might have goals like, "I'm going to contact 10 past clients and see if I can get any feedback on their experience in working with our firm." Make sure you document your progress and then report back to your supervisor.

Weekly Goals Past 30 Days

After you've been with the firm for 30 days, and you've worked through your 30-day Jump Start Plan, you will probably have a better idea of the types of goals you need to set for each week. Have a discussion with your boss about checking in every week and begin to set some longer-term goals with his or her input.

Annual Goals

Setting annual goals at your performance review is a good idea and standard practice for most large companies. If you've been creating weekly goals and reporting on your successes, you'll be in a good place to create yearly goals for yourself. All of this will make it significantly easier to complete performance evaluations and expectations and to show your value to the firm.

SUMMARY

In this chapter, you learned how to create the strategic direction for your firm by using a marketing plan. First, you learned how to conduct various forms of research to educate yourself on the market and then you created a SWOT analysis to determine how your firm can capitalize on its position in the market. Next, you created your Five-Star Marketing Plan which included the following components:

1. Pursuits;
2. Business Development;
3. Public Relations and Generating Awareness;
4. Digital Marketing and Social Media; and
5. Traditional Marketing.

Finally, you learned the importance of Metrics and Reports in tracking your progress as you work your plan throughout the year.

In the next chapter, you'll learn the art of creating great relationships in your business development efforts.

BUSINESS DEVELOPMENT: THE ART OF CREATING GREAT RELATIONSHIPS

 My belief is that communication is the best way to create strong relationships."

Jada Pinkett Smith

Business Development

Excellent business development centers on communication. The most successful business development professionals I've seen are those who are genuinely interested in people and can adapt their communication style to suit the prospect they're targeting. Whether they're selling construction services or designing software solutions, business development professionals are consumed by building great relationships through connecting, consistency, and having a long-term strategy. Below are examples of three great marketing and business development minds and how they approach business development.

One of the best connectors I've seen is Debra Costello. She currently works for a general contractor in Tampa, Florida where she consistently looks for ways to connect people or the key building blocks of making any deal happen. From real estate professionals to bankers to architects to interior designers, there is no obstacle that Debra can't figure out either who to call or what professional to contact to help solve a problem. When asked why has she been successful for more than 20 years, she replies "I'm a people person. I enjoy listening to people in order to understand what kinds of problems they're facing. That's part of how you build the relationship."

Shannon Stein, Business Development Manager for a large Tampa-based general contractor, is not only a great connector, but she is a phenomenal strategist. During the last economic downturn, Shannon stayed focused on maintaining and building relationships with prospective clients she knew would have projects start once the economy improved. When most business developers stewed in negativity about the economy, Shannon continually reached out, stayed engaged, and it paid off in several multi-million-dollar project wins several years later.

"Business Development is like poker. The more chips you put out. The more you get to call back at some point in time," says Anoopa Jaikaran, Marketing Director for a Tampa civil engineering firm, "It might take you years to call those chips back in. But people never forget the good that you do for them and they also never forget the bad." She recommended that marketers just beginning their careers should "Do as much good for as many people as you can, because positions will change, roles will change, people will change companies, but people will never leave the industry. And one day, when you are also in another position for a different company and a different role, they'll remember that you helped them once, and they'll return the favor. In short, think beyond your role."

Getting Started in Business Development

After completing your 30-day Jump Start, you have several tools at your disposal that will help you as you begin doing business development for your firm. You've spoken to previous clients, so you have an idea of why your firm has been successful and what types of clients you should target for the future. You have a better idea of the mix of your clients as well, which may include either or both public and private sector clients.

You've created a short pitch, so you know how to answer the question, "What do you do?" And hopefully, you know how to answer this question in a way that won't bring tears of boredom to the eyes of those you want to impress. Armed with these tools, you're ready to attract new clients. Let's get started!

Business Development Phases

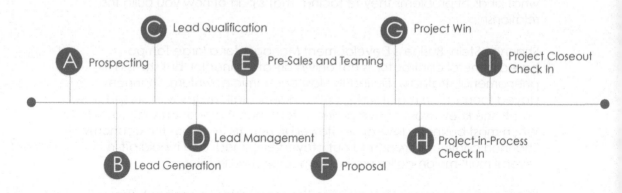

4.0 - Business Development Phases

Start Connecting

If you've ever done real estate or multi-level marketing, you've probably heard of the "Center of Influence." Your Center of Influence (COI) in some circles will be your friends and family, but your COI can also be a group of professionals that you're connected to that can refer business your way. If this is your first job out of college or you've recently started in a new industry, your Center of Influence might include your friends and family. As nice as these people probably are, they are probably not the ones who are going to be able to refer a future project to you. It's time to start a new circle in your current industry. A great way to start creating a new network or Center of Influence is to join three types of organizations:

1. A marketing organization to help you improve your skills;
2. An organization that focuses on training professionals in the service your firm provides; and
3. An organization that targets prospective clients.

Make sure that you attend two or three meetings at each organization before you decide to join. You want to make sure you try different types of meetings within the organization to see if it's a good fit for your needs. Attending meetings in person is very important. When you're selling a professional service, people are buying how you and your team do what you do. The quality of service is important, but professionals want to work with people they like working with. It's hard to start building profitable relationships through digital means alone (email and social media). Meeting people face to face is very important to establish trust and credibility.

Marketing and Business Development Organizations

One of the best professional services marketing and business development organizations you can join is the Society of Marketing Professional Services (SMPS) www.smps.org. SMPS is exclusively focused on marketing professionals who do exactly what you do. At SMPS, you will find marketing coordinators, marketing managers, business developers, principals, owners, and chief marketing officers from architectural, engineering, and construction firms throughout the United States. In the 30-Day Jump Start Plan, I recommended reaching out to some of the board members, and if you've already done that, then you're probably already thinking about joining. You can also do some internet research and find other local marketing organizations in your area. Since your membership in an organization impacts your firm's success, your firm should pay for it (don't be afraid to ask).

Once you've started connecting to people in your local SMPS chapter or other marketing organizations, you may want to start checking in with them periodically (once a month or once quarter). Sometimes you may learn about upcoming projects they're working on or other relevant industry information. The goal is to start forming professional relationships with these contacts. They don't have to be your best friend but it doesn't hurt to have a network of professionals who do what you do daily and can help mentor you in marketing and business development. You may also want to take your professional connections a step further by following them and their companies on LinkedIn and Twitter.

Professional Organizations

Depending on the type of service your firm provides, you may want to connect with people in a few professional organizations to start learning more about the trade you're selling. It's easy to find organizations you should be connecting with by searching online, checking out LinkedIn Groups, and getting recommendations from Principals at your firm. For example, if you work for an architectural firm, you may want to attend a few American Institute of Architects (AIA) meetings by checking out www.aia.org and finding the nearest location to you. If you work for a civil engineering firm, you may want to visit the American Society of Civil Engineers (ASCE) website at www.asce.org. In some cases you may bump into competitors. That's okay. When you're working in a service-based business, you're probably going to run into your competitors many times. I have pretty good business friendships with some of my competitors. When markets change, you never know when you might have to team with a competitor for a project or when you might be in a position to hire someone from a competing firm who just got laid off. Either way, it's good to participate in these organizations to learn about what's going on in your industry.

Prospect Organizations

After completing your 30-Day Jump Start, you probably have a good idea of the markets your company serves. To find these types of organizations, you'll need to do a little more internet research. If you firm designs a lot of retail centers, you may want to check out the International Council of Shopping Centers (ICSC) www.icsc.org. ICSC has a lot of conferences throughout the year in many markets. If your firm does construction for office interiors, Commercial Real Estate Women Network (CREW) www.crewnetwork.org may be a good organization to join. You may get a client from one of these organizations eventually, but the main goal is to find partners that can refer you business.

The Goal Is Quality Connections Not Quantity

In this phase of the game, we're talking about finding people who you can connect with on a regular basis and people who may be able to refer business your way (and vice versa). You're looking for contacts you can check in with once a month or once every two weeks to see what they're seeing in their business. This means you need to have a fairly large COI to work three to five contacts a day, or 60-100 contacts you can check in with each month. If you build a Center of Influence this large, you'll definitely get some referrals without having to be too desperate.

You Have to Give to Get: Working Your Center of Influence

Remember, when you're selling professional services, you're selling how you do what you do as well as what you do. In order to get people to like you and trust you and want to work with you, you need to demonstrate the type of behaviors that make for good team members while you're trying to procure your next client. Always be on the lookout for how you can add value to your Center of Influence. Here are a few ways options:
1. Sharing interesting and relevant industry information;
2. Sharing leads that may be a good fit;
3. Referring contacts when asked;
4. Invitations to an event; and
5. Confidentiality.

Sharing Information

When you did your 30-Day Jump Start, you probably learned about trade publications the professionals in your office checked out on a regular basis. Make sure you continually scan these sources and share relevant articles with contacts in your Center of Influence. By simply calling someone and saying, "Hey, I saw this article and it made me think of the discussion we had a few weeks ago. I'm going to email it to you now," you are staying in contact with someone and sharing something useful. Social media is a great way to stay on top of news in your industry. Just make sure you don't let it take away too much of your time. The most important thing you can do is to use information to connect with people.

Sharing Leads

A lot of civil engineering firms and geotechnical firms are great referral sources for general contractors. These professionals are brought in early and know what's going on far before a general contractor is hired to build a structure on a project. If you're a general contracting firm, you may want to stay in contact with these firms because they may be able to give you some insight. If you're a civil engineering firm or a geotechnical firm, it's a good idea to stay connected with a few general contractors because usually once construction starts, a developer is looking to get started on their next project. Timing is everything and knowing where a prospect might be in their decision-making process is invaluable. Depending on the type of service you provide, make sure you understand the project lifecycle.

When it comes to the public sector, stay informed on the budget cycle for most government agencies. This information is useful for just about everyone in the A/E/C industry that pursues government work. If you pay attention to Capital Improvement Plan budgets, you can share information on what types of projects have been funded to those partners you like working with best. You don't have to share with everyone: be selective.

Referring Contacts When Asked
The more relationships you can establish, the better. Always make an introduction when you can if it will be beneficial to both parties. Don't get in the habit of making introductions just because you were asked. You want to be strategic in who you make introductions to and you also don't want to wear out your relationship with your best contacts.

Invitations to Events
It's a lot easier to attend a professional event with a friend or business acquaintance. Stay informed on upcoming events in your industry and if you have the budget to do so, invite someone from your Center of Influence. Of course, a prospective client is always a first choice, but a well-connected member of your Center of Influence is a great next choice.

Confidentiality
Confidentiality can come into play while working your Center of Influence. I've helped a few people in my Center of Influence find new positions. This takes some careful discussions with trusted individuals. When you earn people's trust and you start learning more confidential information about people and situations, it's good to be known in your circle as someone that can keep a confidence. Relationships work when there is value in both directions and where trust is maintained.

Etiquette

If you're doing business development for your firm, you will most likely be attending meetings outside of the office. It's a great way to make people feel comfortable and more open to sharing information about themselves. You'll probably find it helpful to know a few etiquette pointers focused on successfully incorporating out-of-office meetings into your toolbox. If you're new to business development and haven't taken a lot of clients out to coffee or lunch, here are a few suggestions for the first initial call to set up the meeting, who pays, what food to order or not order, and what to talk about.

Presenting Well

Good etiquette starts with presenting yourself well. It's a first impression that can leave a lasting impression. Presenting yourself well doesn't necessarily mean wearing a suit or a dress every day (although it doesn't hurt). Presenting well means you show up for every appointment 10-15 minutes early and wait in the car if need be so you won't be late. It also means that you know how to show up and be professional. It doesn't matter if five minutes before the meeting you just had a terrible phone call with your husband, wife, girlfriend, or boyfriend. When you show up for a meeting, you're smiling, confident, and "looking forward to meeting with" whoever you're meeting with. Always being "on" is the best way to set your company apart from others.

Phone Calls

No matter who you talk to at a company, make sure you're polite. There is nothing wrong with not knowing who the correct person is to talk to if you know the polite way to ask for information. For example, if you're calling a prospective client and you want to know who would be the best person to talk to, just ask the receptionist.

> "Good morning, my name is Chaz Ross-Munro with ABC Company. I'm interested in finding out who handles land development and planning for your company. Who would be the best person to talk to about that?"

Don't bother saying things like, "I'm so sorry to interrupt you," or "I hope I'm not bugging you, but..." The bottom line is you've already interrupted them by calling so you might as well be prepared with your question. Call the main line between 8 a.m. and 5 p.m. and be specific in how the person at the other end of the line can help you. Once you get the correct person on the phone, make sure you mention who gave you the referral.

How Often to Contact

I think A/E/C veteran Louise Ellrod, says it best: "You have to be professionally persistent." What that looks like depends on the product or service you're selling. If you're always polite, contacting someone once or twice a week via phone and email is okay. After three to four weeks of no response, I might put them on an every three month follow-up plan.

Who Pays at out-of-the-Office Meetings

Whether it's coffee or lunch, the person who asks for the meeting should pay. Depending on how well you know the person you're meeting with, they may offer to pay as well. If you're taking out a public sector client, you may want to ask ahead of time if their agency is particular about who's allowed to pay for lunch.

Breakfast and Lunch Meetings

When you mix nerves with a little bit of lunch, it's the perfect recipe for mishaps. I've attended plenty of meetings where I've spilled things on myself, walked out with most of the food stuck between my teeth, or dropped food on the plate midway between bowl and mouth. When this happens (it will), just laugh it off. It's happened to everyone. I've discovered a few tips for ordering things that may cause the least amount of mishaps:

- If you're at all nervous, stick with water and avoid caffeine.
- If it's a breakfast meeting, make sure you either eat or have coffee (if that's your routine) before you get to the meeting. The purpose of the meeting is to interact with others. If you show up hungry and dragging from lack of coffee, it's not the best way to make a good first impression.
- Always order food that requires a knife and a fork. Anytime I order something to eat with my hands, I run into someone I know who wants to shake my greasy hand.
- When deciding which silverware to use, remember to start from the outside and work your way in.
- If you don't know which water glass or bread plate to use, do this gesture under the table to remind you: The "b" on your left hand is for "bread," and the "d" with your right hand is for "drink."
- Salads can be tricky. A tomato caprese salad is easy to eat with a knife and fork. Other salads can cause mishaps.
- Stay away from soup unless you're a pro and don't slurp while eating it.
- Always pass items to the right (bread basket, dressing, etc.).

Evening Events and Alcohol

If you are attending an evening event, many of the suggestions mentioned above still apply. Hors d'oeuvres and alcohol change things a little in that you want to make sure you bring cash to an evening event in case there is a cash bar or a tip jar. When it comes to hors d'oeuvres, skip them. While you're networking, you don't want to be occupied with the thought that you have something on your teeth or unable to shake someone's hand because you're juggling appetizer plates.

Once the drinks start flowing, topics of conversation will change from some of your daytime events. Make no mistake, evening events share the same business focus that your daytime events do, but the lines can get a little blurry with a few drinks involved. Limit yourself to two drinks: one during networking and one during the dinner (if there is one). If you never drink, don't start at evening events.

Small Talk

Small talk is a fantastic skill to have. If you have it, great. Stop here. If you don't, here are a few suggestions. Always make sure that you listen to what the person is saying and don't try to get out your next question before the person you're talking to is through sharing. It's good to get your guest or prospect to talk about themselves first. If they're shy, don't force it. During the first part of the meeting, try to get your guest to talk more than you do. If you're at a lunch meeting, you can talk a little more once the food comes to give your guest a little time to eat. This probably goes without saying, but here are a few suggestions for topics:

- Instead of talking about what foods you're allergic or have adverse reactions to, talk about the kind of food you enjoy or meals you enjoy preparing.
- Instead of talking about politics, talk about relevant industry trends that may interest your guest.
- Instead of talking about religion or your church, talk about your company philosophy and the HOW of your company – why your company does what it does and why it loves it.
- Focus on what you have in common with the other person. You can also find out more about where they've traveled, where they went to school, hobbies, and their career path (but don't get too personal).

Other Small Talk Suggestions

If the topic of business etiquette fascinates you or you're a little socially awkward like me, Peggy Post's book "The Etiquette Advantage in Business" is a great resource. A few additional suggestions she offers include:

- Familiarizing yourself with multiple topics (i.e., local, national, and world events, as well as sports teams);
- Ask people for their opinions and if you don't agree, use a phrase like: "Actually, I don't agree with you about that, but I'd like to hear more of your opinion;"
- Focus on the person talking to become a better listener; and
- Practice by speaking with all kinds of people you may interact with on a daily basis: Uber drivers, customer service representatives, or the UPS driver.

Hugs or Handshakes
It never hurts to be a little on the formal side until you're more comfortable with someone. Typically, a handshake is always a nice way to say "hello." If you're not a hugger, that's okay. A warm smile and a handshake is always a good way to go. Practice your handshake with friends to make sure yours isn't bone-crushing or a limp noodle.

Handwritten Notes
Some people might think the handwritten note is a thing of the past but it's one of the best things you can still do to show appreciation for a meeting. In the digital age, receiving a handwritten note after an initial meeting pushes past the deluge of email most professionals receive and inspires a little bit of appreciation for the effort.

Introductions
At some point while you're out and about meeting people, you'll run into other people you know. It's always good to know how to make a great introduction. If someone stops by while you're having coffee or you're at a networking event with a prospect, make sure you know how to introduce the person in the most uplifting way possible.

> For example: "Hi Joe! It's so good to see you. Let me introduce you to Betty Smith. Betty owns one of the premier retail development firms in the Tampa Bay area. Betty, this is Joe Blue. Joe does business development for one of the best general contractors in the southeast."

Leveraging Existing Clients and Talking to New Clients
In your 30-Day Jump Start, you spoke to a few clients your supervisor may have recommended. Now it's time to go a bit deeper. Get a list of all the clients your company has worked with in the past year. Based on the amount of time you have, work the list of companies and try to schedule a short meeting with each client to find out how he or she enjoyed or

didn't enjoy working with your company. Before you contact the client, make sure you let the respective project manager who worked with the client know that you'll be contacting them to get this information. Your goal is to introduce yourself, get to know the client, make sure they're happy, and to see if they might know someone else who could use your services. A nice way to close a meeting is always, "Thank you so much for meeting with me, and by the way, would you happen to know anyone else that can use our help?"

Work the Deal Around the Deal

If you haven't heard of "The Advanced Selling Podcast," check it out when you're riding in your car. On episode #406, "Stir Your Sales Funnel," Bryan Neale mentions "working the deal around the deal." I think this is a great suggestion. Even if the clients you met with couldn't give you any direct suggestions on who you can contact, you could try connecting with them on LinkedIn and doing a little research on who your clients are connected to and if there are some opportunities to contact these possible prospects as well. For example, if your firm works in higher education, start reaching out to other higher education contacts your client is connected with.   When I do this, I usually reference the fact we have done work with a colleague of theirs and was curious if they might need our services as well. If your client did not refer you, do not say that the client referred you. Simply say "We're working at the University of Tampa and we thought that since they're growing, you might be as well, so I thought I'd reach out to you."

Being "Professionally Persistent" While Cold Calling and Emailing

Most business development and sales professionals hate cold calling. They prefer instead to do "warm" calls. If you can get a referral from your Center of Influence or a previous client, that is going to make your first call a whole lot easier. In the event you can't make it a warm call, then at least be "professionally persistent" as Louise Ellrod, the Vice President of a large Southeastern general contractor, likes to say. You don't have to be the cheesy sales person, you just have to be polite and persistent. Be prepared, it's going to take you at least 10-15 phone calls mixed with emails to get a meeting with a prospect. Depending on the services you sell, it could take a couple of years. In the A/E/C industry, marketing professionals usually count on 18 months to three years to break into a new market. Although owners will always want you to do it faster, make sure that you're clear on the fact it's going to take some time, especially when you're selling a service and not a product. People have to learn to trust you and your company.

What to Say and How to Say It

If you feel like you need a little more coaching on the business development and sales process, I would suggest checking out the Advanced Selling Podcast's "All In: A Comprehensive Training Solution for Elite Salespeople." This is a series of audio files and email templates that take a lot of the fear out of initiating contact with prospective clients (https://advancedsellingpodcast.com/products/). I think you'll also enjoy listening to Bryan Neale and Bill Casky; they're a lot of fun to listen to.

Transitioning from Business Development to Sales

So you've been working your Center of Influence by reaching out to three to five people a day, you've targeted three markets, and you've been forming relationships with clients in those markets. You've started setting appointments with clients. You have a few meetings scheduled. What do you need now?

Remember, a first meeting with a prospective client is not a marriage proposal. Your goal at a first meeting is not to walk away with a client. If you do walk away with a new client, congrats. But more than likely, it's going to take you a while to earn a new prospects business.

Transitioning from Business Development to Sales

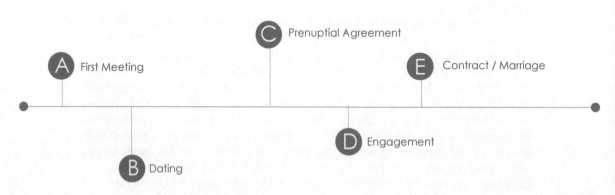

A First Meeting
B Dating
C Prenuptial Agreement
D Engagement
E Contract / Marriage

4.1 Transitioning from Business Development to Sales

Let's Date

At the first meeting with a new client, you're going to want to have a general brochure, but stop with that. Often, I don't bring a brochure to a first meeting. I look at meetings with prospective clients as a first date. If I would have shown up at that first date with my husband with a brochure on my best qualities and why he should pick me as a girlfriend, I probably would have lost him right then and there. However, when business development and sales professionals continually show up with the brochure in hand and start talking about how great they are, they often have one meeting with a target prospect and one meeting only. The way I look at it is that I don't know the client yet. I've reached out to them, I've done some research on the company's website, LinkedIn, etc. But I don't know what specifically this client might be looking for. So, my first meeting is just an introductory meeting. I'll usually prepare some questions about the company. I want to know how the person I'm meeting with fits into the organization as a whole. My goal in that first meeting is to listen. In that first meeting, I want to get the prospective client to talk as much as I can. Some probing questions I might ask are:

- How did you get started in this industry?
- What vendors are you currently working with?
- Why do you like working with them?
- What kinds of vendors annoy you?
- Is there a process to follow to get work with your company?
- Do I need to be prequalified?

I think a first meeting is a success when I have an 90/10 ratio where the client was talking 90% of the time and I was talking 10% of the time. At the end of that first meeting, I simply want to know how often can I follow up with that client and how best to follow up. If a client tells me they don't have any projects going on for the next year, I'll ask them if they mind if I just do a quick email or phone follow up call quarterly just to see if anything has changed. If the prospect is agreeable to that, I'll follow up with another request such as, if I come across some useful information, may I send that to you as well? I'm trying to establish a way to connect on a regular basis with this client.

During the "dating" phase, I want to make sure I maintain contact enough, so that right before the client is ready to release an RFP, I've had the opportunity to introduce them to one of my project managers and they've started to get to know one another.

Show Me the Money - The Prenuptial Agreement

When you start transitioning from business development to sales, you want to make sure there is money in the deal. At this phase in the process, it's critical that the client has the money to pay you. If you're working for a public agency, you can check the CIP budget to know if there is money for the project. If you're working on a deal for the private side, it might be a little more challenging to verify where the money is coming from and if there is money in the deal. When I worked for a global general contractor, we were not authorized to spend any money on pursuing a deal that didn't have some kind of confirmation that there was money in place to make the deal happen. You need to make sure the you're not taking time away from operations to pursue a deal that doesn't have any money tied to it. Questions to verify budget might sound like:

- "Do you have a budget in mind for this project?"
- "Has your team allocated money towards this project for next year?"

Engagement

When an RFP is released, you're looking at getting "engaged" with the client. If you haven't been meeting with the client regularly and you're surprised by the RFP, then a competing firm likely already has the leg up on you. By the time an RFP has been released, you should have facilitated several meetings with your project manager, lead engineer, or architect. Your job at this phase is just to ensure the discussions keep moving forward. When that transition happens, you've now moved from the business development phase to the sales phase. Now your team and prospective client may not understand the nuances of the process as well as you do, but that doesn't matter. The bottom line is, when your prospective client starts talking to your operations team, there is a shift in the deal and the prospective project is looking more real.

During the engagement phase, you want to make sure you have your proposal materials in place and ready. In this next chapter, I'm going to walk you through everything you need for private and public sector proposals. Whether you have a marketing team to help you or if you're a marketing and business development team of one, the next chapter will help you figure out how to start crafting your marketing materials to win your next proposal.

Lead Tracking and Opportunity Management

Lead tracking and opportunity qualification are two of the most important business development activities that exist. If you want to know where a project goes wrong or the company starts to lose money, it often starts during the lead tracking and opportunity qualification process. In this section, we'll discuss how to track, qualify, and manage leads.

Lead Sources

The best way to make sure you stay on track of opportunities is to continually engage with your Center of Influence (COI) and subscribe to a lead service. After reading the previous sections on creating a COI, you'll find your COI is the greatest source for generating leads and making sure that you don't miss any opportunities that might be best suited for your firm.

Other lead sources can come from services like Onvia (www.onvia.com), Bidsync (www.bidsync.com), IMS (www.imsinfo.com), or countless others. There are many lead services that specialize in the type of work you pursue. When it comes to the public sector, these lead services can be helpful. In the private sector, lead subscription services are typically pretty worthless. Most of the services provide subscriptions that vary based on the region your firm is targeting and prices can range accordingly. Lead subscription services can average $1,500 a year or more.

Qualifying Leads

Not all leads are good business opportunities for your firm. The first step in qualifying leads is to review what has worked for your firm in the past:

- What projects has your firm successfully completed?
- What projects were the most profitable?
- What types of clients were the easiest to work with?
- What projects best align with your firm's skill set?

Armed with this information, you have a much better chance of finding project leads that will turn into successful pursuits and then financially beneficial projects. To help identify whether a lead is a good fit for your firm, I've created the Lead Qualifying Form on the next page. You can download a digital copy from my website as well (www.chazrossmunro. com).

1. Do we have an existing relationship with the client? Or have we met with the client a couple of times before hearing about this opportunity?

YES (1 Point)   NO (0 Points)

2. We have done three to five projects or provided services in the past three to five years exactly like the project or service outlined in the scope of work for a similar contract value.

YES (1 Point)   NO (0 Points)

3. We have great references for a similar project with similar challenges.

YES (1 Point)   NO (0 Points)

4. Our team members have provided services or completed projects similar to the scope of work.
YES (1 Point)   NO (0 Points)

5. We were profitable completing projects and services similar to the scope of work specified in the RFP.

YES (1 Points)   NO (0 Points)

TOTAL POINTS _____

4.2 Lead Qualifying Form

If you score 3 or less, then you may want to do more discovery. A "3" means you need more information from the client so you can learn how to best position your firm and whether this opportunity is the best fit for your firm. If you scored a 4 or 5, then you're in good shape. Keep working the relationship and learn more about what you need to do to establish your firm as the clear choice for moving forward with the project.

Managing Leads

The key to managing your leads is to have a follow-up process. Following up with your leads can be easier with the help of an excel spreadsheet or a Customer Relationship Management (CRM) system if you have one. If business development is one of your primary responsibilities, you always need to know your numbers. If your supervisor stops you on Monday morning at 8 a.m., you need to know:

- How many leads you have;
- The client name and project name of each lead;
- Where each lead is in the decision-making process;
- How long you think it will take until the client is ready to move forward with the project; and
- How often you are following up with decision makers on the team.

Below is a small table that can help you stay organized with your leads. If you want to download a digital version, please go to www.chazrossmunro.com.

Start Date	Client or Company Name	Project Name	Estimated Project Value or Size	Lead Phase	Desired Project Start Date	Notes or Follow-up Method
06-15-2016	Company A	A Special Project	$230,000	Shortlist Presentation	06-01-17	Presentation scheduled for February 2017
07-15-2016	Company B	B Special Project	$400,000	Proposal in Process	01-30-17	Proposal 90% complete
07-21-2016	Company C	C Special Project	4,000 sf	Proposal in Process	02-30-17	Proposal 70% complete
08-22-2016	Company D	D Special Project	5,000 sf	Discovery	03-30-17	Follow-up every 30 Days
08-24-2016	Company E	E Special Project	$1,000,000	Discovery	04-30-17	Follow-up every 30 Days

4.3 - Lead Management Sheet

Stay Focused

Great lead qualification can be a key factor in determining how profitable your firm is by only pursuing those clients and projects that are the perfect fit for your firm's capabilities. Spending time on pursuits that you're not qualified for will only erode profits and patience within your organization. If you are laser-focused in the types of pursuits you go after, your chances of winning increase exponentially.

Teaming Arrangements

When you market and sell professional services, you have a wide variety of referral opportunities open to you. However, you can only tap into these opportunities if you are extremely focused on what your firm does well and what your firm does better than its competition. If you tout that your five-person firm is a "full-service" anything, you're kidding yourself. You need to figure out exactly what your firm does better than anyone else, so you know how you can look for teaming and partnership arrangements. Firms that do it all are usually the 800-pound gorillas in your industry. Don't try to compete with the full-service gorilla. Instead, look for the best specialists in your industry and team with them.

How to Find Teaming Partners

Sometimes it can be a little challenging for principals and senior project managers to find time to do the necessary networking to find partners. Business development professionals can do the most good in this case when it comes to identifying teaming partners and spending a little time researching them as well. Earlier, I mentioned establishing your Center of Influence and using professional organizations as a way to connect with professionals from other firms. When you're looking for teaming partners, these organizations can be useful.

An even better way to find teaming partners is to ask clients you'd like to work with who they are currently working with. An example of this might be if you're a civil engineering firm, you would want to talk to the facilities department head and a school district you'd like to work in and ask them which architects they like working with and why. Your next step is to connect with these architects and maintain the relationship with the facilities department head. That way when a project comes up with the school district, you've worked both sides. The department head now knows your firm and the architectural firms know you're a good teaming partner because you have a relationship with district already.

Do Your Research

Before you enter into any teaming arrangement, you need to make sure you really know who you're getting into bed with (so to speak). Although you may not be able to request financials from a teaming partner like the municipal procurement departments can, there are a few ways that you can determine if your prospective teaming partner is a good fit for your firm. Here are a few ways to check out a teaming partner:

- Do an internet search on your teaming partner. You'd be surprised what you can find if you do a couple of internet searches on a company and its principals. Although there is no such thing as the perfect partner, make sure you avoid putting your business on the line by teaming with a partner that might have some skeletons in their closet.

- Check their social media profiles. You can find out a lot if you review a firm and their key staff's social media profiles.
- Check out Dun & Bradstreet. Depending on the age of your teaming partner's company, they may or may not have a profile on Dun & Bradstreet. Either way, it doesn't hurt to find out.
- How do they treat you? When you've scheduled meetings with a possible teaming partner, do they show up on time? Do they reschedule with you over and over again? Do they do what they say they are going to do? How well do they follow up? All of these factors are very important and show you how your potential teaming partner would be like to work with.

Honesty and Confidentiality

If you're looking for a teaming arrangement for a specific public sector project and your cousin is on the selection committee, it's okay to let people know that you have a good relationship with a prospective client. It's also okay to team with multiple firms on a project pursuit (in most cases). Just make sure you're honest with your partners that you are on other teams as well. In the architectural, engineering, and construction industries, it's standard to see a specialty subcontractor on a variety of teams. What's not okay is for this subcontractor to share confidential information from other prime contractors with other contractors competing for the project. Make sure you are honest and use good judgement in the types of information you share.

Exclusive Teaming Arrangements

Something else you might see in a public sector project pursuit is exclusive teaming arrangements. In some cases, a prime contractor may want to ensure that it has the best possible team and there is no way that information can leak between primes from a similar subcontractor group. Under this scenario, prime contractors may choose to enter into exclusive teaming arrangements with subcontractors. This is usually done as a "Memorandum of Understanding" or "Teaming Agreement," which defines the terms and duration of the relationship for a particular pursuit. This approach is fairly common with design-build projects when general contractors will enter in to exclusive teaming arrangements with architects and other key design professionals. Many times, these arrangements are created long before an RFP is released for a specific project. That's why it's very important that your firm does a solid pre-sell approach before the RFP is released (more on pre-selling in the next section).

Team to Grow
Finding the right teaming partners can serve as a great resource for growing new project opportunities for your firm. Make sure you take the time to find the best teaming partners through your networking efforts. Research and meet with appropriate teaming partners to get to know them better, and then enter in to the best arrangements that offer the best opportunities for your firm.

Pre-Selling
When you did your marketing research and reviewed a few Capital Improvement Project (CIP) budgets, you probably identified a few projects that aligned with your firm's expertise. If that's the case, now is the time to work on pre-selling the project.

What Is Pre-Selling?
Pre-selling is forming a plan to secure a project for your firm. This process can also include a discovery phase. For example, after doing CIP research, you learned a municipality has money allocated for a new $6 million IT system. You would get to work pre-selling by setting meetings with department heads to ask them more specific questions about the existing system, the problems it has, and why the municipality is looking to revamp the system.

You also need to find how the municipality determined a new system would cost $6 million (this municipality could already have a consultant in place that has a better strategic position than your firm to win the project). Based on this information, you could begin to determine the best strategy for winning this project when the RFP comes out. Depending on where the department is in creating the RFP, you may have several months in which to meet with the department heads periodically to gain more insight on the challenges involved with implementing the new system for the municipality.

Also, it doesn't hurt to follow A/E/C Marketing and Business Development veteran Carol Scheafnocker, "When you are doing your business development, do your research on who actually sits on the selection committees. Get to those folks and find out what each of their hot buttons are. If one says written communication, another says they don't want change orders, and another wants the project to come in under budget, make sure each of these are addressed with proof in the RFP as well as in the presentation."

Why Pre-Sell?

Usually large, complex projects with the high fees require a top-notch approach to winning over a prospective client. You must begin to establish a relationship with the client before the RFP comes out especially if you are a new company to the client. In the public sector specifically, a government agency is not going to spend $6 million on a project with a team that has no proven track record. Therefore, most winning pursuits begin with a solid business development approach way before the RFP is released so that department heads have an opportunity to get to know your firm's project team. When the department heads or selection committee know your firm and feel like your project team understands their concerns, the proposal you submit will carry a lot more weight.

Forming Teams Starts During the Pre-Sell

As you're working on the pre-sell for a project, that's when you want to start working on your teaming arrangements. In the previous section, you learned about what you need to look for in a teaming partner and how to find teaming partners. After you've met with the prospect and you know more information about the project, it's a great time to start looking for the best partners to round out your team. Conversely, if the opportunity isn't the best opportunity for you to be the prime contractor, start looking for other firms you can team with on the pursuit.

Should You Pursue an Opportunity with No Pre-Sell?

You really shouldn't pursue an opportunity that you didn't pre-sell or adequately perform discovery. A lot of times during the discovery/pre-sell process, you uncover a lot of information that won't be included in the RFP. There is always information that doesn't make it into the RFP which could have a huge impact on your firm's pricing and project strategy. Although there is usually a question-and-answer period in most procurement processes, at this point it's too late to make significant changes to a project and pricing strategy and still be competitive. When I've seen a contractor submit a bid on a project they did no pre-sell on, they usually have a hard time determining an appropriate pricing or project strategy because they lacked awareness of the entire scope of the project through a proper pre-sell and discovery phase.

Stack the Deck in Your Favor

Pre-selling really helps to stack the deck in your favor. When you take the time to do adequate pre-sell and discovery, it greatly impacts your chances for a successful project pursuit that results in a win. With adequate discovery, you can ensure that you appropriately price the project. A great price and a fantastic approach are the result of making pre-selling part of your business development process.

Maintaining a Happy "Marriage"

Once you've secured a client and are working on a project, how do you make sure your clients stay happy? Like any relationship, consistent and regular communication will help maintain a healthy relationship. In this section, we'll talk about how to stay in touch during a project, once a project wraps up, and maintaining the relationship until the next project comes along.

During the Project

After your business development and proposal efforts have paid off, you want to ensure that the client stays happy throughout the duration of the contract. It's important that the business developer and the project manager come to a consensus on how often the business developer will touch base with the client to make sure the client's expectations are being met (this duty can also fall on the shoulders of senior management as well). The project manager should be aware of how and when the business developer will be contacting the client. If the client feels like there isn't good communication between business development and project management, it may create tension on the project. Depending on the type of project, frequency of contact with the client by business development will vary. If a project is scheduled to be six months long, checking in three times would be appropriate: one month after the project starts, in the middle, and the close-out survey.

During a project, the business development professional can be the most useful. Since he or she isn't typically involved with the project, the business development professional can ask questions and receive feedback in a way that doesn't become uncomfortable for the client. For example, if a project is not going as well as the client likes, having a business development professional check in and get feedback without having to directly speak to the project manager might be easier for the client if the client has a good relationship with the business development professional.

It is absolutely critical that the entire project team - including the business developer - keep the client's interests in mind. With that said, the point of the project check-ins isn't so that business development can go and tattle on the project management team to senior management. The purpose of checking in during a project is to keep the project on track and make sure that if a client is unhappy, the client's issue can be resolved before it becomes too late.

Project Close-out Survey

After the project is over, it's a great time for the business developer to take the client out to gain more feedback on what the client liked about the project and what the client didn't like about the project. I really like taking the client outside his or her office so that the survey seems less formal (taking the client out to coffee or lunch is a good idea). The most important thing about the close-out survey is to make sure the client feels comfortable giving their feedback. You really do want candid feedback: it will help your firm grow. The questions asked during this phase can be simple and straight-forward:

- What did you think went well on the project?
- What did you think didn't go so well on the project?
- What can we do differently next time?
- Do you have another project coming up we can help with?

Coaching the client after each response with phrases like, "Thank you for your feedback, can you be more specific about this aspect you mentioned [fill in the blank]," will glean fantastic insights. This is also a great time to ask if the client would be comfortable giving a letter of reference. Offer to write the letter based on the feedback received during the close-out survey, it's a great way to show you listened!

Following Up

In between projects, following up is a must. Consistency is key and you don't have to spend a lot of money in most cases to maintain a great relationship. Here are a few suggestions:

- **Thank You Gifts.** Depending on the size of the contract your firm just completed for a client, something as small as a handwritten note is always nice. However, if the contract was fairly substantial, put some thought into a nice gift for the client. Edibles are always a nice idea (especially at the holidays), but feel free to use what you know about the client and company to select the appropriate gift.
- **Seasonal Gifts.** I'm located in Florida. I worked for a firm that used to send out a little bit of "warmness" during the winter months to their northern clients. The gifts were small and thoughtful and made a great impact on existing clients.
- **Handwritten Note.** Many business developers choose to plow through the digital noise by going old school and sending handwritten notes. I still think this works. If you find an article or a piece of news that might be useful to a client, print it out, and mail it to them with a small note, "Just thought you might find this interesting. Hope all is well!" It doesn't take a lot, it just has to be useful and relevant.
- **Events.** If you run in the same circles as some of your clients, chances

are you'll bump into them at a local event. Instead of making this a chance meeting, you may want to offer to pay for their attendance. In Chapter 12, I'll talk more about tournaments and educational events. These types of events are great ways to stay connected to clients.

- **Promote Your Clients.** Celebrate your clients' successes with them. We live in the digital age and if your clients are sharing their stories via company blogs, Facebook, Twitter, and LinkedIn, make sure you help them share their stories. Connecting with your clients on their social media is a great way to reinforce relationships. Be careful how you connect, though. While following a client on LinkedIn and Twitter is a great way to start, Facebook can be too personal initially.

Sales Is Every Employee's Job
A prevailing thought in some professional services firms is that marketing and business development professionals solely bear the responsibility for bringing work into the firm. Unfortunately, in this competitive age, marketing, business development, and sales is not just one person or few people's job - no matter how energetic they are. Thanks to social media, every individual at a firm is now an ambassador for your firm's brand.

Firm leaders can't expect the efforts of a few marketing or business development professionals to be enough to remain competitive. From the CEO to the janitor, everyone is involved with making money for the firm and is also responsible for making sure your clients are happy. So how can you make sure an attitude of "clients first" prevails through your firm?

Onboarding
Not only is the 30-Day Jump Start Plan a great way to integrate marketing and business development professionals into your firm's culture, but it's a great way to onboard all of your employees. Each employee has a network that he or she can tap into and help your company sell more work. If you sell professional services, then so much of what you do depends on relationships. Every employee can help you expand your network and also help your firm find its next project. Your employees are a great lead-generation system. Use it and reward it! Experienced marketing and business development professionals can help coach your employees on how to turn leads into sales as well as following up on leads that come from existing relationships. Transparency, and an attitude that operations can work with marketing to bring in work, is critical.

Reward Service Focused Behavior
Does your firm reward its employees for bringing in leads, serving existing

clients well, and looking for ways to be helpful to their team members? If not, now is a good time to start. Selling your brand starts with selling it internally to your employees. Sometimes in professional services firms, employees get so focused on getting the job done that they forget to be appreciative of each other and celebrate internal successes. Birthdays and anniversaries matter. Professional services firms that focus on serving their own people and celebrating their successes will promote similar positivity outside the workplace. Have you ever met someone who says they love their job and feel appreciated by their company? Usually your next question is, "Are they hiring?" Make sure your firm has rewards in place to help celebrate your employees - or make a suggestion for the firm to start.

Communicate Your Values

Internal email newsletters that promote examples of how your employees are going above and beyond are a great way to show your employees you notice their good work. In a service-based business, your employees are your firm's calling card. When your employees feel appreciated, they will transmit these same good feelings to your clients, which will in turn reward your firm with more work. Documenting case studies of client problems that your team members worked together to solve is great content for internal and external newsletters. When you communicate your team's successes in email newsletters and social media, it really helps solidify the idea that your employees' good work is noticed and appreciated.

Have a Good Lead-Generation Program

If your employees refer a lead to your marketing and business development team for an upcoming project, make sure you reward them for it! Although some people are happy to contribute with no reward, it doesn't hurt to have a reward program in place. If an employee refers a lead that turns into a project, a $25 gift card is a nice gift; if it's a larger project, offering a referral bonus isn't a bad idea either. The bottom line is, you hired most of your employees to do a specific task that wasn't directly related to sales. If you want your employees to keep an eye out for profitable opportunities, you will encourage them when you show appreciation with a gift card or a pat on the back.

SUMMARY

4

In this chapter, you learned how business development is the art of creating great relationships. You also learned:
1. How to set up a center of influence and connect with professionals in meaningful ways to build your referral base.
2. The different phases and ways business development can assist with the sales and project cycle.
3. Lead qualification, teaming, and pre-selling opportunities.

In the next chapter, you'll learn more about preparing the materials you'll need to educate your clients and sell your company's services to clients.

5

PRE-PROPOSAL PREPARATION

 I feel that luck is preparation meeting opportunity."

Oprah Winfrey

Telling Your Firm's Story

When you meet Michelle Casale, it's hard not to smile with her. She has a vivacious smile and brings an exuberant energy to every project she works on. I've had the pleasure of serving on the Tampa Bay Society of Marketing Professional Services Board with her for a few years. Michelle is a storyteller for a top general contractor in the Southeast. She knows how to weave the story of her company into her proposal narrative in seamless and creative ways. Michelle is the type of marketing manager who is always looking to improve on her past successes and always looking for new creative inspiration, "I love putting a proposal package together and telling our story."

Michelle is also an expert at leading complex project teams with a variety of sub-consultants to craft winning proposals, "When you work on a proposal, you get to work with every team member, different skill sets, and a diverse range of personalities. After 15 years, I still love that! I've lead teams of more than 50 sub-consultants and that's enormously powerful knowing I can do that."

It is Michelle's drive and "can-do" attitude that makes a challenging endeavor a feat easily achieved with some prior planning and effort. In this section, I'm going to give you a few best practices that Michelle and some other top-professionals in the A/E/C industry use to manage the proposal process. If you do the proposal preparation outlined in this chapter, you'll be able to tell your company's story in a compelling way that will help drive more work to your business.

What Are You Selling?

Since you're working for a professional services firm, you're going to need documentation that illustrates your experience and the strength of your team. Since you don't have a "product" per se, creating a tangible way to illustrate the value of your firm to targeted clients is important. In this section, I'm going to talk more about how large firms procure services through a process that usually involves a document called a Request for Proposal or RFP. Later in this section, I will give more specific information on the different types of documents that aim to do the same thing: give information in a format that helps your client make a decision.

Building a Proposal Content Library

In this section, you're going to learn how to take a lot of the information you started gathering during your 30-day Jump Start Plan and turn it into collateral pieces that help you sell your company. I'm going to teach you how to create project or experience sheets for your firm, resumes for your team, and a company overview. These documents will help you better understand how your firm has helped its clients in the past and what kinds of projects your firm is qualified to take on for future business. When you're working for an accountant, lawyer, software engineer, or general contractor, it's hard to sell professional expertise unless you really understand the types of challenges they help their clients solve. By taking some time to create this documentation, you'll build a library of content that can help you respond to an RFP or any question a prospective client has about your company.

You Don't Always Have to Start from Scratch
Some of the information you'll need to start writing proposals may already exist. If your company has hired a full-time or part-time marketing person like yourself, chances are they may already have a website that has much of the information you'll need. If they hired you to help create the website, then the team members you interviewed during your first few weeks at the firm will help you gather a lot of the information you'll need.

What is the Purpose of RFPs?
As projects grow larger in both scale and budget, the number of decision makers involved in the project grows as well. In order to make evaluating vendors easier, procurement specialists use the RFP process to make evaluating proposed solutions with multiple decision makers easier. A RFP (or Request for Proposal) can be issued by a government agency or a private company. The RFP usually has: a company overview, summary of the problem or solution the agency or company is seeking, a scope of work, and a list of questions or functionality requirements for the proposed solution. The purpose of an RFP is for a government agency or private company to create a standardized method to procure services and goods from contractors such as yourself. RFPs usually have tight deadlines. To meet RFP deadlines, you must have your firm's material and research completed ahead of time (which is what the rest of this chapter is all about).

Definitions

Agencies may also come up with their own acronyms for RFPs. The requirements may be based on each agency's own terminology. In most cases, if an agency issues a document that ends in a "Q," then it usually means the agency is seeking a qualifications-based response only, and is not requesting a pricing component at this time (but make sure you confirm this with the agency if you're unsure or the RFQ is unclear). Throughout this book, we'll also use "RFP" as a blanket term for standard procurement forms listed below:

- RFQ - Request for Qualifications or Quote
- RSQ - Request for Statement of Qualifications
- RFI - Request for Information
- SOQ - Statement of Qualifications
- ITN - Invitation to Negotiate
- ITB - Invitation to Bid

Project Sheets

Every RFP is trying to determine if your company is the best provider for the service and can do so at a reasonable cost. Simple, right? The best way to prepare for an RFP is to have several types of materials already prepared so you don't spend 90% of your time looking for the information and only 10% putting it together. We're going to try to flip that ratio through this process. I want you to have 80% of your materials ready to go, so you only have to spend 20% of your time writing customized material. So let's talk about how to do that.

What experience do you have providing the product or service the agency is looking for? What types of similar projects have you done in the past? This is where you start. Let's say you own a painting company and you want to get a job with the ABC County School District. You know a school in the district is getting ready to remodel a portion of the school and that there is going to be a huge painting contract. You want it. To prove that you deserve the opportunity, you need to gather some relevant project information.

PEPIN ACADEMIES

Project Start
2011

Project Completion
Ongoing

Reference Information
Dr. Joe Smith
Principal of Pepin Academies
3916 E. Hillsborough Ave.
Tampa, FL, 33610
Phone: 702-561-9191
Email: jsmith@theacademies. us

RSA Project Team
George King

"The Pepin Academies has celebrated over 15 years of excellence in education, with over 80% of the students graduating with a standard high school diploma and 20% on track graduating with a special diploma."

BACKGROUND
Founded in 1999, with the help of the Pepin Family, Pepin Academies are 501(c)(3) not-for-profit, tuition-free, public charter schools dedicated to the educational needs of students with identified learning and learning related disabilities.

Today, Pepin Academies has grown to serve over 850 students, with a main campus in Tampa, a campus in Riverview and its latest addition in New Port Richey, serving the students in Pasco county.

SUPPORT PROVIDED BY RSA
RSA assists the Pepin Academies by providing a variety of marketing, public relations, and community outreach services. RSA's services range from event planning, media relations, and public outreach to managing board meetings, setting agendas, and on-boarding key staff and board members. RSA also coordinates each year their High School Students' trip to Tallahassee to meet their legislators and learn about public policy during Session. RSA monitors all legislation related to charter schools and directly advocate for legislation that would benefit the Pepin Academies.

5.0 Project Sheet Example

The best project sheets have several pieces of information:
1. **Project Name.**
2. **Start Date.**
3. **Completion Date.**
4. **Amount of Contract.**
5. **Image depicting the work done on the project.** If you do renovation work, before-and-after shots are a great idea. If you don't do any renovation work, any project photo will do. If you sell a service like web development, use a screenshot of the website.
6. **Project Description.** A good project description has three components:
   A. Where or why the project was completed;
   B. How your company was able to complete the job better than most of your competitors; and
   C. How your result made your client happy and solved their problem. In our painting example above, the project description might sound like, "The ABC project was a residential project which involved painting two 8 x 11 rooms that had extensive drywall damage and peeling paint. Joe Smith's Painting Company examined the existing surfaces and determined extensive drywall work would be required to give the walls the finish the homeowner desired. Based on Joe Smith Painting Company's established relationships with vendors in the community, our firm was able to save the homeowner $350 by using Super Duper Drywall Mud without compromising the desired result.
7. **Project Reference.** Make sure you can get a reference from your project client. Basic information you need to collect is:
   A. First Name
   B. Last Name
   C. Company (if there is one)
   D. Address
   E. Phone Number
   F. Fax Number (Yes, a lot of agencies still ask for this and it's okay to say NA if one doesn't exist.)
   G. Email Address
8. **Project Team.** Name the team members who worked on the project and each person's role on the project.

As you can probably tell, that's a lot of information to collect and keep track of. You're right. But, the best part about a comprehensive project sheet is you can re-use it again in some of your other marketing materials.

Resumes

Slaving over your resume is definitely not the most fun task when selling to a new employer. When you're contracting with a city, county, or state agency, that's just what you have to do, though. Except in these cases, you are now presenting your professional experience instead of an overview of all of your capabilities. Brevity is important but so is selling how you and your team is the most qualified to complete the work outlined.

Most RFPs are going to ask very detailed questions about your staff and your previous experience in providing the service you are selling. In addition, you want your resume to outline in detail how you have completed projects similar to the proposed project you are bidding on.

Make sure that you have spent the time doing the project sheets so that you have a lot of the information ready for the experience portion of the resume.

1. **How Should I Organize This Information?**
2. **Name and Project Title.** Each team member should have their name and project title clearly listed at the top of the page. Note that I said "Project Title." If you are a team of one, then your company project title wouldn't be president (although that's true). Your project title would be "Project Manager." This is important because the department heads want to know who is going to be managing the project and the key point of contact. It is very important that the agency really understands what each team member will be doing during the project.
3. **Education and Training.** A lot of times, team members graduated with a degree that may not have any relevance to what the person is doing now, which is fine if it's a degree from an accredited university. Training certifications are very useful. If you are the proposed project manager for a project, make sure you list if you are APM certified. If you have other relevant certifications to the project you are bidding on, make sure you list those as well.
4. **Professional Organizations.** Are you a contributing member to the profession you're a part of? If you're a civil engineer, are you a member of the state engineering society? If you're a general contractor, are you part of the local AGC or ABC Chapter? If you're a marketing organization, are you part of AMA? If you are, make sure you list these organizations as well.
5. **Role Description.** Make sure you give a very detailed description of what specific tasks the individual will be accomplishing on the project. For example, if the resume is for a project manager, they may be

responsible for overseeing the successful outcome of the project, ensuring all necessary resources are available on a daily basis, and serve as the primary point of contact for the customer. It is very important that you outline here exactly how the team member will be serving the client.

6. Experience Overview or Bio. Here you want to summarize how the person you are proposing in the role is uniquely qualified to perform the services needed. If you are listing someone as a project manager, it is important that they have a track record of successful projects. A good overview will discuss how many years the person has been a project manager, if they have any additional training to make them a great project manager, a quote from a previous satisfied client testifying to the abilities of the project manager, and a brief summary of their skills.

7. Project Experience. Here you want to list all the project experience the team member has that is relevant to the project you are proposing this person for. It is a lot easier to build a resume when you have a company resume. By working on the project sheets before working on the resumes, you now have a great portfolio of company project experience to pull from.

Since we're working on this resume BEFORE the RFP is released, we may be uncertain about some of the project specifics. It doesn't hurt to categorize the project experience if the person has performed services for multiple market types. For example, if the project manager is for a small software development firm, you may want to organize the experience under categories such as, "Government," "Industrial," "Healthcare," or "Municipal." You want to capture the following information for each project: name, start, completion, role of the person on the project, brief description of the work completed for the client. You want to keep the project description firm-focused since you already outlined in the Role Description what the person listed on the resume will be doing for the project. You want to use projects where the individual held the same role as the role you plan on proposing them for in the future.

Nick DeMelas Project Manager

Professional Skills
Windows 8
Server 2008 (and R2)
Vista
XP
Server 2003
Mac OSX
iOS
Linux
HTML
XHTML
CSS
PHP
MySQL Microsoft SQL-Server
JavaScript
Visual Basic
C++
Oracle

Professional Experience
14 Years

Education
B.S. Management
Information Systems
University of South Florida
Tampa, FL

Summary of Experience and Role on Project
Nick has 14 years of experience in project management, database design, programming, IT systems design, and training. For the Tom's of Maine project, Nick will be involved with the following:
- Discovery - Nick will assist in creating wireframes and documentation for the technical aspects of the project.
- Development & Implementation - Nick will oversee development of the entire front and back-end which consists of the core application logic, databases, data and application integration, API and other back-end processes.
- QA / QC - Nick will perform testing and debugging of the front and back-end applications and system.
- Maintenance and Support - Nick will be one of the designated support engineers assigned to the Tom's of Maine project for the duration of the contract.

Relevant Project Experience
Crosstree Capital Partners Website and CRM integration
Client: Crosstree Capital Partners
Role: Project Manager
Description of Project: Sourcetoad created Crosstree's online systems which included: a customized CRM solution; web sites; portals; CRM integration with web lead management; and backend business intelligence systems. Contract value: $250,000.

Viking Cruiseship Entertainment System
Client(s): Viking and RedCell Technologies
Role: Project Manager
Description of Project: Sourcetoad has created a suite of software solutions for Viking's in-cabin entertainment and content delivery systems. Viking's software suite is an end-to-end solution, which includes: set-top video players in cabin; the kiosk and digital signage systems; content management backends; and the middleware layer for integrating pre-existing assets into the network. Contract value: $1.3 million.

5.1 Resume Example

Company Overview

You probably have most of what you need for a company overview on your current website in the "About" section, but it won't hurt to have this information in a branded Word document so that you've got it ready to go at any time. Since most RFPs will be submitted in PDF form, it doesn't hurt to have some presentation-ready handouts that have a general company overview about your organization.

Length

A company overview should be no longer than two pages. Chances are, you may not use all of this information most of the time. The purpose of having a longer document is to have the content ready. It's always easier to cut content out when you're on a short deadline than trying to create new content in a rush.

Content of a Company Overview

What is your company about? What kinds of clients do you work with? What kinds of problems do you typically solve? These are all questions your prospective clients may have and having some canned or boilerplate material is very helpful to have handy to address some of these questions.

Some other questions you want to answer in your company overview are:
- How many years have you been in business?
- Who are the key staff for your firm?
- What are your specialties?
- What is your service offering?
- Do you have any client testimonials? Make sure you include them here!

Highlight the Best Projects and Case Stories

Do you have any project spotlights for your firm? Your company overview is a great place for these. Any specific project highlights you can list will be a huge benefit and add credibility to your organization. Instead of using general comments like, "We create solutions that save our clients money," you may want to try verbiage like, "We created an energy-efficient office building that reduced energy expenditure by 20%, saving our client more than $20,000 in operating costs in 2015."

Third-Party Testimonials

You could do all of the talking on your company overview, but sometimes it's even better to have someone sing your praises for you. Client testimonials are a great way to enhance your company overview and are better than any ad or marketing brochure.

Summary of Your Team and Locations

Your company overview is also a great place to insert a picture of your team. Is your company very large or does it have multiple locations? Your company overview is the perfect place for an organization chart or map that details where your other office locations are.

Firm Services

What do you do? That's a pretty standard question to answer at most dinner parties. But when you're trying to explain in more detail how you help your clients through the services your company provides in a way that differentiates you from your competition, that presents a challenge.

Start with the types of problems or pain points you help your clients with and work from there. If you sell website consulting services, you might hear problems like:

- Why does our website look weird on a desktop monitor or a phone?
- I can't update my website on a regular basis because I don't know how to code so it costs me a fortune.
- How do I make my email templates and website have a similar branded look?

After you've answered a couple of these questions, it gets remarkably easier to write content about your services.

Why does our website look weird on a desktop monitor or a phone?
- **Responsive Website Design.** *Websites now have to display properly on a variety of devices and a variety of screen sizes. It's important that your website looks great on each one. At ABC Development, we can update your website so it's responsive or adjusts accordingly to a variety of digital devices and screen sizes.*

I can't update my website on a regular basis because I don't know how to code so it costs me a fortune.
- **Content Management System (CMS) Consulting.** *Most businesses utilize a content management system for their website so they can update information regularly without having to learn how to write HTML or CSS. ABC Development can help you set up your website on a CMS that makes sense for your business.*

How do I make my email templates and website have a similar branded look?
- **Custom HTML/CSS Template Design.** *It's important to have a consistent brand among your social media and web digital assets.*

ABC Development can help you create a consistent digital brand by designing customized HTML/CSS templates so your website and emails look brand compliant and consistent.

Depending on your services and the complexity of the services you provide, a few sentences is usually enough for each type of service.

Company Approach

Do you have a consistent method you use to solve your clients' challenges? Many proposals ask for a specific method or approach of how you will work to solve their problem. The best project approaches have six components:

1. A summary of the benefit your solution provides.
2. Restatement of the client's problem and challenges.
3. A detailed explanation of your solution and how it solves the client's problem.
4. Resources and techniques that will be used to solve the problem.
5. Timeline or schedule to implement the solution.
6. The benefits your solution provides.

Even though you're writing this before you have a proposal, you can write about the type of problems you typically solve. Depending on the type of problems your company solves, your approach can vary in length between one and five pages.

A Summary of the Benefit Your Solution Provides

Make sure you address how you're going to make your client's life easier in the very first sentence of your approach. If you own a civil engineering firm, you may solve a lot of different challenges for a lot of different types of companies. You can still summarize the benefit of your solution by talking more about how your company works to solve problems. For example, "CRM Civil works with healthcare, higher education, and retail companies expanding rapidly in Hillsborough County. We have more than 20 years of experience working with the County to help our clients move through all phases of design and permitting as quickly and as efficiently as possible." Immediately your prospective client is thinking, "Great! They can save me time and money because they are familiar with the County." That's exactly what you want them to think as you take them through the rest of your approach.

Restatement of the Client's Problem and Challenges

In this section of the approach, you want to restate what challenges the client is facing. You may think this is repetitive, and it is, but it shows that you're listening to your prospective client. Use the language the client uses. When I'm writing a general approach, I'll usually refer back to a previous RFP and see what kinds of statements a client makes in the scope of work. Remember, we're just coming up with a general approach framework here. This is what you'll add to once you have a real RFP sitting in front of you. If you have pictures that document the types of problems you typically solve, make sure you use those here.

A Detailed Explanation of Your Solution and How It Solves the Client's Problem

Do you have a five-step discovery process you use to analyze a client's issue? Do you have a 20-step quality control process to meet specific standards? This is the part of the approach where you discuss these processes in detail. Again, graphics or images that are specific to your process are helpful here. Sometimes, I like to include screenshots of sample reports or images of successful outcomes.

Resources and Techniques that Will Be Used to Solve the Problem

At this point in the approach, it's a good idea to give more information about your team members and the benefits each of them bring to a typical project. Depending on the size of your firm, an organizational chart may be helpful. Following the organizational chart, you want to write a sentence or two about each member of the senior management team. If you work for a small company, it's okay if you skip the organizational chart and just do short bios for each team member.

Timeline or Schedule to Implement the Solution

Clients always want to know how long something is going to take. Although you may not have a project yet, you can start to plan within your approach for this type of question by having your process broken down into a Gantt chart or a table. The simple Gantt chart below has milestones broken down by weeks. If you don't want to do a Gantt chart, you can use a simple table as well with key milestones.

Schedule of Deliverables

*All dates will be determined and confirmed at kickoff meeting.

Milestone	Week 1	Week 2	Week 3	Week 4
1. Start	▓			
2. Kick-off Meeting	▓			
3. Database Development / Testing		▓		
4. Concept Approval		▓		
5. Critical Review Meeting			▓	
6. Test Plan Review			▓	
7. Test Readiness Review			▓	
8. Acceptance Review				▓
9. Operational Readiness Review				▓
10. Website Launch				▓

5.2 Gantt Chart with Deliverables

Schedule of Deliverables

*All dates will be determined and confirmed at kickoff meeting.

Item	Date	Milestone	Description
1	TBD	Start	Signing of contract.
2	TBD	Kickoff Meeting	Data gathering and database discovery, connection, collection.
3	TBD	Database Development / Testing	Database development begins using data collected during discovery.
4	TBD	Concept Approval	Feasibility studies and basic system concepts have been agreed upon management and the project is authorized to proceed to detailed requirements definition.
5	TBD	Critical Review Meeting	Requirements specifications are complete, correct, approved and suitable for input to begin design process and the development of code.
6	TBD	Test Plan Review	Test plans are adequate for the testing of all product features, are approved and are suitable for input to the development of test cases and test procedures.
7	TBD	Test Readiness Review	Developed and unit tested software has been passed by the test team and is suitable for input into integration testing, alpha.
8	TBD	Acceptance Review	The website has passed system testing and is suitable for input into acceptance testing, beta.
9	TBD	Operational Readiness Review	The website has passed acceptance testing and is suitable for deployment in its target production environment.

5.3 Table with Milestones

The Benefits Your Solution Provides

At this point in the approach, it's wise to restate the benefits of your solution. Since we're writing a general approach, you may want to use another testimonial from one of your clients that talks about an experience with your firm and how it benefited them.

Proposal Information Management Matrix

As you can see, you need to gather quite a bit of information to make sure you're ready to assemble your RFP response. Perhaps one of the best ways to ensure you always have accurate project experience and up-to-date resumes is to set up a Proposal Information Management Matrix. In the process I've outlined below, I use a simple Excel spreadsheet to track what information the marketing department has and what information is still needed from project management. Perhaps the most useful aspect of this process is it gives senior management a quick way to see what information the marketing team is missing.

On the next page, you'll see a basic Proposal Information Management Matrix. This matrix has specific project information milestones:
1. Project Manager (PM) Completes Information Form;
2. Project Sheet Created;
3. Rendering of the Project (or project image);
4. Approval for Rendering or Stock Image;
5. Final Project Sheet Completed; and
6. Reference Letter Obtained. You'll note that I used 1s and 0s depending on whether the item was completed, which gives me an overall score for how up-to-date my proposal library is.

Project Name	PM Completes Information Form	Project Sheet Created	Rendering of the Project	Approval for Rendering on File or Stock Image File	Final Project Sheet Completed	PM Final Project Sheet Approval	Reference Letter Obtained	Total
Red Project	1	1	1	1	1	0	0	5
Orange Project	1	1	1	1	1	0	0	5
Yellow Project	1	1	1	1	1	0	0	5
Green Project	1	1	1	1	1	0	0	5
Blue Project	1	1	1	1	1	0	0	5
Purple Project	1	1	1	1	1	0	0	5
Black Project	1	1	1	1	1	0	0	5
White Project	1	1	1	1	1	0	0	5
Complete								40
Total								56
% Completion								71%

5.4 Proposal Information Matrix

Project Name

Once you've won a project, make sure you are consistent with what you call the project. I know this seems like a small detail, but when you start trying to dig for information in multiple systems (i.e., accounting, marketing, etc.), if a project is called one thing in one system versus another thing in a different system, it starts to create a lot of confusion.

One way to head this issue off from the very beginning is to make sure marketing and finance agree on what the project (and subsequent phases) will be called. Once you have a new project, this jump starts the rest of the process.

Project Manager Completes Information Form

In a perfect world, you would send a project information form to a project manager and he or she would complete the form with no hesitation and have it back to you ASAP. That won't happen. Chances are, you are going to need to sit down with the project manager and discuss the project and get them to help you fill out this form. This information is important. You will use it to generate the next part of this process, the Project Sheet. Not all of the information that you get for a project sheet should be communicated externally outside the office to clients, but it's good for you to capture this information while it's still fresh in the project manager's mind. When you pursue government projects, you will sometimes need to list fee information. You can always put "confidential" but it will be important for you to determine during your pre-sell or during the question-and-answer portion of the procurement process whether listing "confidential" will throw you out of contention for a project.

Project Information Form

Project Name

Project Start

Estimated Project Completion

Design Fees

Construction Costs

Client Reference Name
Client Reference Company
Client Reference Address
Client Reference City / State / Zip
Client Reference Phone
Client Reference Email

Project Team Member 1
Project Team Member 2
Project Team Member 3

Description of Project

Services Performed

5.5 - Project Information Form

Project Sheet Created

Once you have the Project Information form filled out, it's much easier to begin to draft a Project Sheet. If you go to my website (www. chazrossmunro.com), you can download a Microsoft Word version of a project sheet template. You may need to customize it based on your industry. If you work for a software engineering company, you will want to include screen shots of the project. Having all of the information you need on one sheet will help you with your next qualifications or proposal package. You can always delete information, but sometimes on a tight deadline it can be one more challenge to get a project manager or other professional to give you pertinent information when you need it. This process ensures that you have this information ready ahead of time.

Rendering or Stock Image for Project

An image is worth a thousand words. A great way to brand your project is to find an image that represents the work your firm is doing. If you work for an architect or construction firm, get a rendering of the project to place on your project sheet. If you work for a software engineering company, you may want to use the wireframes. Either way, anything you can get to graphically represent the work you're doing for a client is a great idea.

Approval to Use Rendering or Stock Image

If your company created the rendering or wire frame images, then you're in good shape and you don't have to worry about this step. If not, you want to make sure that you get approval to use renderings or stock images. If you send an email request for approval, make sure you get authorization from an officer in the organization. If you buy an image from a stock photography website, just make sure you get an image that's royalty free and keep the purchase receipt on file. You can get sued for using images that don't belong to you. If you use an image that you found on Google, you can get fined for this as well. I wouldn't risk it. Although buying stock photography can be a little expensive, it's much cheaper in the long run than getting sued for using an image that doesn't belong to you.

I recommend the following stock photography websites:
- iStock (www.istockphoto.com/)
- Think Stock (http://www.thinkstockphotos.com)
- Adobe Stock (https://stock.adobe.com/).

Progress Photos

Another alternative to using renderings or stock images is hiring a photographer or taking photos yourself. If your firm is a design or construction firm, taking progress photos and incorporating those into your project sheets is a great way to create a bigger impact from your marketing materials. Quality is important and if you're not the best photographer, hiring a professional can make a big difference. Hiring a photographer can also be expensive so depending on the project size, you may want to hire a professional for your bigger, more high-profile projects. Depending on the size of the project, you can also work out arrangements with photographers so that you can split the costs, but you must get approval from the photographer.

Final Project Sheet

Once the project is completed, double check all of the information on your project sheet. Go back to the project manager and verify the information and see if anything has changed.

Letter of Reference

Immediately after your firm has finished a project, ask for a letter of reference from the client if it was a successful project and the client is satisfied with your firm's performance. Do not request a letter of reference by email or phone and then forget about it, thinking that it's as important to your client as it is to you and your firm. If you take this approach, you will never get a reference letter because, chances are, your clients are fairly busy. Offer to write a letter of reference for your client and use the information you've collected for the project sheet as a basis for the reference letter.

SUMMARY

In this chapter, you learned how great proposal responses start before the RFP is even released. Maintaining your proposal library requires a fair amount of work and follow up with project management. If you continue to maintain your proposal asset library, it will make a huge difference when it's time to submit a proposal. You'll be able to find the information that you need quickly, which will, in turn, help you to focus more on key win themes for your proposal.

In the next two chapters, we'll talk about two different types of proposals: pubic and private. In both chapters you'll start to apply what you've learned about proposal preparation to help you win your next private or public sector project.

LETTER AND PRIVATE PROPOSALS

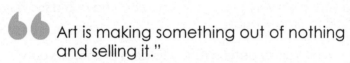 Art is making something out of nothing and selling it."

Frank Zappa

Introduction to Private Proposals

The art to writing a great proposal is answering this one simple question: "So what?" The true "proposal artists" out there can clearly illustrate the value of their services in a way that really sets their firm apart from competitors. JR Kozera, the Business Development Manager for a global engineering firm located in Tampa, FL, responded to this issue: "I used to work with a marketing manager who would say, 'So what' whenever you wanted to add a particular piece of content to a proposal or presentation. Basically, she was trying to get you to see why it mattered to a client."

Making sure that your proposal is always on point with what matters to the client is the one factor that separates a winning proposal from a losing one; writing a concise document that can quickly illustrate your value to prospective clients is simple but not easy.

An Approach to Private Sector Proposals

Don't waste time submitting a proposal on work that won't help grow your business. You can save yourself a lot of time by building some standard questions into your discovery process. If you don't have a discovery process, it's time to create one!

Chances are, when you're getting ready to do a proposal, you've already started to do some light discovery into what the client may be looking for in a solution. Before you sit down to write a proposal for this type of client, make sure you've answered several key questions. Again, get these questions answered before you start writing a proposal. Writing a proposal takes time away from your core business functions and it's important to spend time on work that will profit your firm.

Budget

Does your client have a budget in mind? This will greatly affect the type of solution you offer to provide. You'll be surprised how many professional service providers begin writing up a robust solution for a client that is in no way shape or form within the budget living in the client's mind. Make sure you don't waste the time writing up a solution before you have investigated what the client's budget is and then reverse engineer from that number.

Timeline for Completion

Does your client have a specific timeline for when he or she would like the work completed? This may affect your fee structure. Based on the client's timeline, you may also decide that it's best not to submit a proposal.

That's okay, too! When you're deciding what work to pursue, make sure that you don't take on projects you can't do well (or have no chance of getting). It also helps to have other firms you can refer these types of projects to if they're not a good fit for your company.

Reporting and Deliverables

Based on the type of service you're providing, you need to establish how often you need to communicate with a client so he or she feels they are receiving a great value for the service you are providing. During your discovery process, you can ask questions like: "How often would you like me to contact you about the project once we begin?" and "What methods of communication are best for you?"

Contract Component of the Proposal

In your proposal, you may have a contract. If you don't have a standard contract you use in coordination with your proposal, stop now and go see a lawyer. Do some research on contracts used in your business, create a document using some of these key components, and then talk to a lawyer about creating a contract that ensures you are protected. I know all of this seems basic, but it's extremely important.

If you already use a contract, you may be rolling your eyes at this point. However, when did you last have your service contract reviewed? If you have been in business for a few years, I'm confident your business has changed since you first got started. It's good practice to review your contract every few years to make sure it still offers you the protection you need.

Format of Your Proposal

Keep the format of your proposal simple if the client doesn't specify anything. Generally, proposals have the following components:

1. **Overview.** Create a sentence or a couple of paragraphs describing the project or problem the client is facing.
2. **Approach.** Summarize the approach and services you'll use to address the project or problem.
3. **Services.** Clearly describe the services you'll provide.
4. **Schedule.** If the project will take longer than 30 days to complete, you may want to give a detailed breakdown on each of the service components and how long they'll take.
5. **Fees.** Make sure you present your fees in a way that is easy to understand for the client.
6. **Contract.** Insert your contract.
7. **Signature.** Create a place for a signature for both parties.

Proposal Tools

There are many proposal-generation tools you can find online based on the type of service you provide. I'm all for most technology tools but when it comes to proposals, I recommend keeping it simple. The last thing you want to do is frustrate a business owner who is trying to give you their business. Create a standard proposal on a Word document. Before you send the document to a client, create a .PDF file and then email it.

Follow Up

Make sure you follow up on your proposal. It never hurts to check with your prospective client when he or she may be looking to make a decision.   Follow up by calling and emailing until you get a decision. There is a delicate balance between following up and stalking. If a client tells you 30 days, I'll usually follow up within 25 days and then every week after.

6.0 Private Proposal Example (pages 1-2)

Approach & Pricing

Overview
As we look at the HOST program, we envision a three-year approach to getting the program up and running. This includes one year of research and development, then two additional years to get five schools up and running with the program. As we move into years two and three, we can also assess a broader rollout plan for the program that will take us beyond our intitial three-year contract term.

Our three-step process to assess, develop, and roll out the new program will all take place in year one. Years two and three are to ensure the program consistently achieves the desired goals.

The five schools targeted for the new program include:

1. **Frost Elementary School**
   3950 Falkenburg Road
   Riverview, FL 33578

2. **Ippolito Elementary School**
   6874 S Falkenburg Rd
   Riverview, FL 33578

3. **Nelson Elementary School**
   5413 Durant Rd
   Dover, FL 33527

4. **Pinecrest Elementary School**
   7950 Lithia Pinecrest Rd
   Lithia, FL 33547

5. **Limona Elementary School**
   1115 Telfair Rd
   Brandon, FL 33510

Three-Step Process
The three-step process we'll use to improve the HOST program is:

1. Evaluation & Assessment (3 Months)
During this phase, we will research the current system in place and interview all team staff members currently managing the afterschool program.

2. Curriculum Development and County Review (6 Months) During this phase, we will formulate our plan for th...
review/pr...
their com...
staffing, a...
externally...
address t...

3. Progra...
At this phα...
curriculu...
by all key...
implemen...
elementa...

Pricing
Each yea...
program ...

Year 1 - $...

Year 2 - $...

Year 3 - $...

PHASE	2016				
	Aug	Sep	Oct	Nov	De
Phase 1 - Evaluation & Assessment					
Phase II - Curriculum Development & County Review					
Phase III - Program Rollout					

Our Team

Team Overview
BSAC strives to not only meet state mandated guidelines, but exceed them when it comes to training and developing our staff. Each of our proposed team members is state-licensed, and receives 20-30 hours of additional training when hired to ensure he or she meets BSAC standards.

Chuck Burgess | Executive Director
Chuck Burgess will serve as the Project Manager and oversee the entire implementation of the new after school program during all three phases: evaluation, development, and rollout.

Chuck has a strong background in education and was a former Seminole County Teacher of the Year. Also, while teaching for Seminole County, Chuck was part of the curriculum writing team for elementary and middle schools.

Chuck has served as the Executive Director for BSAC for the past six years for BSAC and has successfully led the organization to its most stable position in its 50-year history. Chuck

has served twice as the Brandon Rotary Club President and also serves as President/Owner of Impact Management and Consulting which serves both the NPO and for-profit sectors about organizational health, change management, strategic development and top-level leadership development.

Additional Team Members and Their Role on the HOST Curriculum Consulting Project
- **Christie Lemar - Youth Development Director.** Christie will be responsible for assisting with the organization, delivery, and quality of the after school program for students in Kindergarten to 5th Grade. Her primary focus is to provide a positive experience for students by managing and coordinating with school advisors.
- **Shelby Johnson - Assistant Development Director.** Shelby will assist the directors with organization, delivery, and quality of the after school program.
- **Kim Dearth - Director of VPK and Early Childhood.** Kim will be responsible for assisting with the organization, delivery, and quality of the after school program for the VPK and Early Childhood students.
- **Vanessa Davis - Site Director.** Vanessa will be responsible for the oversight of the day-to-day operations of the after school program, including: planning, coordination, and supervision.

Proposal to Provide Consulting Services to Hillsborough County Public Schools
Submitted by Brandon Sports & Aquatic Center

Page 3

6.1 Private Proposal Example (pages 3-4)

SUMMARY

In this chapter you learned how to conduct enough discovery before the proposal is requested by a client to ensure you have enough information to pitch the best solution for your client's project. Next, you learned how to properly format your proposal with all pertinent information. In the next section, we'll go more into proposals for the public sector. But first, we'll take a quiz to see if you're ready for the public sector!

7

READY FOR GOVERNMENT WORK?

 Before everything else, getting ready is the secret of success."

Henry Ford

Readiness Quiz

Working in the public sector is challenging. In order to help you avoid spending a lot of time and effort in an area that may not pay off for you, I've developed a "Government Procurement Readiness Quiz." The quiz is an objective tool to help your firm decide if it's ready to pursue city, county, or state government proposals. If your company isn't really interested in going after public work, you can skip this section. If you're unsure of whether government work might be a good fit for your company, make sure you review this section first and then you'll have a better idea of whether you should pursue this type of work.

If you don't score more than 80% (eight points) on the readiness quiz, you may want to revisit some of your proposal preparation materials before attempting to go after city, state, or county contracts. Following the quiz, I explain why you need to consider each factor more carefully before pursuing government contracts.

Government Procurement Readiness Quiz

Government Procurement Readiness Quiz

1. Has your company been in business for at least two years? And does it have a back log of at least 6-12 months?
   Yes (1 Point) No (0 Points)

2. Has a key person in your company worked with or for the city, county, or state agency your firm is targeting? Or do you have a good relationship with a department head you'll work with at the city, county, or state agency?
   Yes (1 Point) No (0 Points)

3. Does your company have a clean bill of health (please select "Yes")? If your company doesn't pay its bills on time, the company has been sued, or the president of the company have any type of legal issues, please select "No.")
   Yes (1 Point) No (0 Points)

4. Are you willing to spend 10-16 hours researching government agencies you want to pursue? Or do you have someone that can do the research for you?
   Yes (1 Point) No (0 Points)

5. Have you looked at RFP responses from a similar service or product you offer with the city or county agency you're pursuing?
   Yes (1 Point) No (0 Points)

6. Are you willing to do cold calling and schedule meetings with government procurement professionals and department heads? Or do you have someone who can do these tasks for you?
   Yes (1 Point) No (0 Points)

7. If you qualify, are you willing to spend 10-20 hours preparing SBE and WBE applications?
   Yes (1 Point) No (0 Points)

8. Are you willing to spend 60-120 hours preparing materials you'll need to submit for an RFP or have resources that can help you?
   Yes (1 Point) No (0 Points)

9. If someone on the street stopped you, could you list one to three key differentiators as to why the product or service you provide is the best in the industry?
   Yes (1 Point) No (0 Points)

10. Do you have a documented process for everything you do in your company? If someone asked you to write detailed instructions of how you do everything you do in your business, could you do it?
    Yes (1 Point) No (0 Points)

How Long Have You Been in Business?

When I was 12 years old, I took gymnastics at Parkway Gymnastics. We practiced in a small gym at Carmen Trails Elementary School in Manchester, Missouri. Since I had been going to Parkway Gymnastics since I was eight, the coaches knew my maturity and skill level pretty well. Parkway needed a coach for an after-school program teaching gymnastics. It was a great start for a first job. Since I didn't have previous experience as a coach, I got to learn through trial and error. I loved it!

After coaching the after-school program for several years, I heard from a fellow coach that I could make a little more money at a larger gym in the area. It required a little work to get certified, but the money was worth it. Since I was getting close to driving age, this seemed like a great idea to earn some extra money. So, I decided to apply for the position at the larger gym and take the necessary certification courses. The certification program did a couple of things: first, it gave the coaches a baseline understanding of how all of the gyms within the organization were run; second, it detailed the fundamental rules for running a class; and third, it shared safety guidelines to mitigate any risks of injuries or lawsuits. After taking the class, I felt a lot more confident about running a class and what was expected of me. I also had a greater understanding of the risks involved if something went wrong. The stakes were definitely higher when I was coaching at a larger gym.

I share this story with you because, until now, you've probably gotten a lot of your first jobs the way that I did. You knew a few people who knew you had expertise in a particular area. You leveraged these relationships to get some of your first jobs. Over time, you developed a reputation for providing excellent service and have grown your business to a substantial size. You probably didn't have to undergo any kind of formal certification process. People knew your reputation, trusted you, and gave you the job. However, selling to a government agency is a little different and requires a similar type of certification program.

When you're selling to a city or county government agency, you're selling a product or service that the taxpayers are paying for. During the procurement process, the government is going to ask for a few things that you may not have had to provide in the private sector to determine whether your company is stable enough to provide services or products to the scale required by the government agency. Based on what type of product or service you provide, you're going to have to come up with the following documentation: (1) documents of incorporation, (2) two or three years of tax returns, (3) certificates of insurance, (4) small business designations, (5) W-9, and (6) Bonding Capacity (contractors only).

Documents of Incorporation
One of the first documents you'll need to have on file is your documents of incorporation or proof of business status. It can be incredibly difficult to track these documents down if you don't already have them when trying to prequalify or submit an RFP response.

Tax Returns
Agencies want to do business with stable companies that have little to no risk of providing the product or services they are contracted to complete. Based on the size of the contract or the agency, you'll need to provide two or three years of tax returns.

Certificates of Insurance
After you've read this book and you've found an opportunity you want to pursue, trying to obtain a certificate of insurance may be a pain. Make sure that you have the necessary qualifications to obtain a certificate of insurance before you see the first opportunity. Sometimes obtaining the proper insurance can take longer than the amount of time you have to complete the proposal or statement of qualifications.

Small Business Designations
We'll talk about these later in this chapter.

W-9
If your company has been in business for a couple of years, chances are you've completed a couple of W-9s for the various firms you've worked for.

Bonding Capacity
If you provide construction services, you will need to be bondable (If your firm doesn't perform construction services, don't worry about this part). Do you know what your bonding capacity is? Your bonding capacity will be a determining factor for the size of the projects you will be able to pursue with the agency.

Once you've acquired all the documentation you need to prove to any government agency that you've been in business for a few years, are a stable company, and they can trust to provide your product or service, then it's time for the next step.

Has Someone Worked with or in the Agency You're Targeting?

Government agencies and municipalities are large, complicated organizations. It is extremely useful if you or someone in your firm has some experience in working with a particular agency your firm is targeting. For example, a lot of civil engineering firms will make a strategic hire from a municipality. Hiring someone who has experience with the internal workings of an organization as well as personal relationships with the staff can be a tremendous asset for any professional services firm. Also, before you make that strategic hire (if your firm is considering it), make sure his or her reputation is as good as the person you're trying to hire says it is. I've seen a few firms make a hiring decision only to regret it later. Civil engineers usually do a fair amount of work for municipalities, so the more familiar a particular agency is with the staff of the firm, the more likely they'll be hired to do more work. When you're competing for work in the public sector, not only are you competing with firms that have extensive project resumes, you're competing with previous fellow coworkers as well.

Can't Make a Strategic Hire?

If your firm lacks the resources to make a strategic hire, that doesn't mean you can't still continue to pursue a specific municipality. An existing relationship will speed things along; if you don't have one, it will just take a little more time to make an impact. Make sure you meet with department heads and the procurement specialists at the municipality you're targeting. It may take longer to build a relationship with key staff at the municipality, but it's not impossible. Also, make sure you double check and see if anyone at your organization might have a relationship through mutual acquaintances and friends.

Does Your Company Have a Good Reputation?

Do you have any skeletons in the closet? That's okay, you're not the only one that does. It's not the skeletons in your closet (or your company's closet) that can cause you damage as you pursue government projects, it's not knowing how to handle questions about them that can affect your ability to win new contracts. Before you begin the process of completing your first RFP, make sure you have solid references. You want to make sure that you have both client references and vendor references.

Client References

If you've forgotten what projects you've done for who, now would be a good time to review your invoices and make note of all of the clients you've helped along the way. If possible, try not to use references related to you. You want to position your firm as an established leader in your field, and listing your brother as a client reference (even if you've done work for him) may not represent your company as strongly as a client with another government entity you've done work with. At a minimum, make sure you have this information ready for your clients:

- Name;
- Company;
- Address;
- Phone number;
- Fax number (yes, some agencies still fax things);
- Email; and
- Description of the work you've performed.

Also, make sure you have the client's permission to use him or her as a reference. Even better, get a reference letter from the client. When you ask for a letter of reference, offer to write it for them or offer to give the client a list of the specific tasks and services you provided. Chances are your clients are just as busy (or busier) than you are. Anything you can do to help make the process easier on your client is going to make obtaining a reference faster for both of you.

Vendor References
Some government agencies actually want to know how you are at paying your bills on time and may ask you for a few vendor references. In this case, you don't really need a letter of reference typically, but it's a good idea to have a few names and numbers handy in case they do.

Overcoming Issues with Your Firm's Reputation
If your firm doesn't have a great reputation with an agency or a past company you have worked with, the first step is to find out what went wrong. Employees in your firm probably have their ideas, but you want to get the information directly from the client's mouth. Usually, it's helpful to have someone do the interviewing who hasn't been connected with the past projects and to get this feedback in person. The client will likely be more comfortable and candid if he or she hasn't worked with them in the past.

Before you begin interviewing past clients, make sure senior management at your firm knows you will be conducting these interviews and why. Try to get as much information from the project team that worked on the project as well as senior staff so you are comfortable with the entire back story before talking with the client.

The interview process doesn't have to be lengthy. Try asking these three questions to start:

1. What did you like or not like about working with our company? What do you perceive as the biggest challenges we had on the project?
2. What firms are you working with now (if not us) and what do you like about working with them?
3. What could we do to earn a project with your company again?

Make sure you listen to the responses and ask more follow-up questions, if necessary. The point of this exercise is to get the client to feel comfortable and open up about what went wrong on the project and to re-establish lines of communication. If the client is still angry, then let him or her vent. Apologizing is okay, but don't overdo it. Close the interview process by thanking the client for their time, and ask them if you can contact the client again after visiting with your team and working on some of the issues you discussed during the interview.

After interviewing the client, follow-up with your team and set up a meeting to discuss the client interview and the feedback you received. Brainstorm with senior management to develop ways of improving your company's project management style to better match your client's expectations. Keep the meeting focused on creating a way to improve going forward, rather than a finger-pointing session or blame game. Take detailed notes on all solutions discussed and be ready to present these solutions to your client at your follow-up meeting.

After you have the interview follow-up meeting with your internal team, schedule the follow-up meeting with your client within the discussed timeframe. Remind your client that you're following up (as you said you would) and would love the opportunity to share the changes your organization has now made thanks to their input. You may not get the opportunity to meet with your client right away, but keep following up.

Eventually, the timing will work out and you'll have the opportunity to persuade your client to consider using your firm again. This entire process may take a little time so be persistent.

Have You Done the Research?

The government procurement process (city, county, state, or federal) is extremely time-intensive and expensive. Targeting the right municipalities for your firm to work with is extremely important. Earlier, I mentioned the importance of having a good backlog. Making sure you have the time to research and plan for your first government contract is critical. There are two key factors to consider as you target government clients: location and CIP budgets.

Location
Where is your business owned or operated? If you are located in Tampa, Florida, your first government submittal for work should not be in Los Angeles, California. Your business location is critical when you pursue government work. If your company is based out of Tampa, first, you should research the City of Tampa. Next, you take a look at the county the City of Tampa resides in: Hillsborough County. You can also look at the school district for that county as well. Once you have a contract with City of Tampa, Hillsborough County, or Hillsborough County Schools, you can begin researching other municipalities. The secret is, start close to home first.

CIP Budgets
Is a contract with a government agency worth the wait? It depends. A good way to determine which government agencies you should be targeting is by looking at Capital Improvement Project budget. Hopefully, you started checking out CIP budgets when you were working on your marketing plan in Chapter 3. Every city and county agency has a CIP budget. Your first step in this process should be to determine which agencies have money allocated for the product or service you sell. You should use this information to dictate how much time you spend during the year chasing work with the specific agency.

How Well Do You Know the Competition?
Do you remember in school when sometimes the teacher was nice enough to give you a really thorough review of the content that was about to be tested in the next class?
Fortunately, you have the same opportunity in the public sector to capture great information about what the agency is looking for before you submit your proposal.

If you've been in business for a few years, chances are, you've started to run across a few businesses that provide the same product or service as you. The good news and the bad news is when you're chasing government projects, you have access to a lot of information that could help you be more competitive. Having a clear idea of who your competitors are will really help you in determining what opportunities you should be chasing or what types of work the government agencies think you might be a good fit for.

After determining which agencies you should target based on location and budget, it's time to find out how good your competition is. Thanks to the Freedom of Information Act (FOIA), you may be able to get proposal information from some of your competitors and this can be valuable information if you're new to pursuing public work. This part of the process is relatively simple:

1. Find a previous RFQ or RFP that was for a product or service similar to yours; and
2. Contact the municipality and ask them for a copy or for access to review the submittals.

Each agency is different and some states may differ in how you can access the information. In Florida, you can request this information and the agency will either let you come in and view proposals or send you an email link to the digital copy. Each state and each municipality's process may be a little different.

Pricing

Ever wonder how you stack up to your competition in regards to pricing? Researching previous RFPs is another great way to find out where you stand on pricing compared to your competition. In Florida, you can obtain this information as well if it was contained in the original proposal for services if the service you provide isn't related to architecture and engineering. Per Florida Statute 286.055 regarding the Consultants Competitive Negotiation Act (CCNA), architects and engineers can only compete on qualifications and not based on price.

How to Find a Previously Awarded RFQ or RFP

Depending on how your agency of choice releases its RFQs and RFPs, you will need to do a little digging to find an RFQ or RFP for a product or service like yours. Let's say in this example we're trying to find an RFQ or an RFP for wireless instillation services. I would do some preliminary research on Onvia Demandstar (www.demandstar.com). You may have to set up a free account first if you're not already set up. Next, do a quick search on awarded projects in a specific agency. For this example, I'm using one close to home: Hillsborough County. Next, look for a project similar to the project you're interested in pursuing in the near future. Then, contact the agency and ask them for either an electronic version of the RFP responses if they are available. Some agencies may require you to come in to see the books in person. No matter how the agency is set up, the best thing you can do is review the RFP responses and pick apart what makes some proposal responses better over others. When you take the time to do a little research on past proposals, you will gain valuable insight on how to better position your firm.

In Chapter 10, I'll talk more about the debrief process. In the debrief process, if possible, you want to review other proposals submitted for the same project as well so you can learn what the winning firm did differently.

Have You Introduced Yourself to the Agency?

So now you've reviewed CIP budgets and you know which government agencies have the type of funding that makes it worth your while to pursue them as a client. Now, you need to begin to get to know that agency and work towards building a relationship with them. The first step is to discover nuances in their procurement process. To win your first government agency contract, you need to be very familiar with the respective agency's procurement process as well as what that agency looks for in a possible product or service provider. This can make the entire process very time-consuming unless you have a targeted strategy. Before we focus on the differences, let's focus on the three similar qualities every city and county government agency has in common: (1) A method of distributing RFPs, (2) A standard process for reviewing the RFPs, and (3) A standard process for debriefing after each RFP decision has been made. You'll need to know this process for the agency as well as what the department who will be using your product or services likes in a provider.

Get to Know the Agency's Procurement Process

Now, making sure you understand the procurement process, every government agency (city, county, state, university) has a different procurement process. Some agencies have their own system, where you have to go in, log in and they'll send you bids that they think you're qualified for, or that they're willing to accept from you because of your qualifications. There are other systems where you have to qualify first. Especially if you're a general contractor, you must prove that you even have the bonding capability to pursue some of the work that you want. The best way to make sure that you really understand the procurement process is to meet with someone from the procurement team. During this meeting, ask questions about their process such as:

- Where do you post bid notices?
- What upcoming projects do you have?
- What common mistakes do vendors make when they submit bids and how can I avoid those?
- Do you have a pre-qualification process? If so, how do I complete it?
- Which department, and department head would help make the decisions for the product or service you sell? How would you get in

contact with this person?
- What is your evaluation process like?

Home-Court Advantage

When you're taking the time to get to know your targeted agency, start close to home. Focus on the city agencies in your county and the county agency as well. Don't spend the time driving out to agencies further away until you've won your first contract with the agencies closest to you.

Your Next Meeting with the Agency

After you've met with the procurement department, you want to make your next meeting with the department head. During this meeting, you're trying to discover specifically what he or she and the department is looking for in a good contractor. You should ask questions like:

- Who are you currently working with, why do you like working with them?
- Have you had any problems with contractors in the past? Can you describe what happened?
- Who have been their best contractors? What made them easy to work with?

Meeting with the department head and asking those really good questions will help you build a long-term partnership. Agencies won't hand out a $20,000 deal to a company they're not familiar with. Agencies want providers that can demonstrate their interest in being a long-term partner with the agency. Remember, the only benefit to pursuing government work is not just the work itself. By completing this process, you're getting very detailed coaching on how to win a contract not only with this agency, but with other clients in the private sector as well.

Can You Fill out The Forms?

If you want to go after public work, you must play every card at your disposal. If you're a small, woman-, minority-, or veteran-owned business, there are is an opportunity for your firm to gain extra points on many bids based on your status as a disadvantaged business. Please don't let the term "disadvantaged" discourage you. In many cases, you're going to be competing against firms that have a team of marketing people working to produce proposals to keep their company's pipelines full. It's just going to take a little work ahead of time to get your firm certified.

Are You Registered?

You can't let being small, woman-, minority-, or veteran-owned work for you unless you complete the necessary paperwork. Depending on the agency or institution your firm is targeting, you will need to fill out the requisite forms to certify your firm as the appropriate designation. If you try to register your business once an opportunity comes out, you are way too late. With most designations, your firm needs to be operating for one to two years before your firm can qualify.

If you qualify as a disadvantaged business, make sure that you look for opportunities to team with larger organizations as well. You can't team with larger organizations if you're not registered. If you're going after city and county work, you must be registered with the appropriate status in the city or county you've targeted.

Do You Have the Time to Work on Securing Government Clients?

Your company really needs to have a backlog of existing work before you begin chasing government projects because the timeline to get started is much longer than in the private sector. The government tries to be a good steward of the taxpayer's dollar, therefore, before a large amount of money is spent on a product or service, the agency is going to spend time vetting contractors to ensure the public gets enough bang for its buck.

Although the timeline is long on the road to securing a contract, it doesn't mean you're just sitting around and waiting. When you discover a project you're interested in, you will need to begin to map out a plan to secure the project. This begins with discovering who the key stakeholders or department heads are who will be managing the project on the agency side. You can find out who these people are by asking around, which means starting with the procurement department. This means your first meeting may be with the procurement department, your next meeting may be with the department head, and then you may want to have a subsequent meeting based on what you discuss while meeting with the department head. The purpose of these meetings is to gain familiarity with the agency.

Documentation: How Do You Do What You Do?

Government agencies want to know how you're going to deliver the product or service you're promising to provide in your RFP. Most proposals will probably contain questions that attempt to understand more about your company and how long it's been in business, more commonly called a company overview. Agencies will also want to know if you have a standard process for delivering your services, your methods for staying within budget, and a proposed schedule for how long it will take for you to complete your product or services. Good thing you created most of these in Chapter 5.

What Are Your Differentiators?

If someone did stop you in the middle of the street and ask you what your company does and why they should hire you, could you respond in one sentence? You've probably heard of the classic "elevator pitch," and this question aims to get you thinking along the same lines of the words you choose to sell your business. When you are selling to government agencies, you're not alone. It's often very competitive and you're competing against great firms that have been submitting proposals for years, have earned multiple contracts with the agencies, and are comfortable with the particular agency's procurement process. Since you or your company is new to the process, you really need to understand why your company is different.

WIIFM

Whether it's a public or private client, each one is tuned into WIIFM or "What's In It For Me?" If your differentiator isn't important to your client, then your proposal won't be either. Lee Frederiksen with the marketing consulting firm Hinge offers these three tips when creating a differentiator for your firm (and all can be applied to proposal differentiators as well):
1. It must be true;
2. It must be important to clients; and
3. It must be provable.

Be Different to Be Memorable

When a selection committee is reviewing multiple submissions, a clear strategy to differentiate itself in a positive way from competitors is critical to creating a winning bid. Depending on the client and the situation, you can change how you choose to differentiate yourself. Let's say for a particular agency, I learned in my discovery process that having a local contractor is very important to the agency. The agency has also experienced difficulties with a "one-size-fits-all philosophy" that some of the larger vendors tend to sell over and over again. Since I know (from experience) that two of my biggest competitors support too large of an area to pay this agency a lot of attention, that gives me a window of opportunity as well as something I could use as a differentiator for my firm.

Create Your Differentiator

Now that I know what's important to my client, I need to take a little time to think through what kind of differentiator would be considered true and relevant to the client. Also, can I prove it? It's now time to do competitive research (by going to each of my competitors' websites and find out how my competition talks about themselves). To do that, I'll use a matrix like the one below to help me (go to www.chazrossmunro.com) to download a template).

Website Content Research	My Company	Competitor A	Competitor B
Message A	~~Local presence~~	~~Local presence~~	~~Local presence~~
Message B	~~>20 years experience~~	~~>20 years experience~~	~~>20 years experience~~
Message C	One location.	~~Multiple locations throughout the~~ region.	~~Multiple locations throughout the~~ country.
Message D	Use ABC products, XYZ products, or whatever product client would like	~~Only uses XYZ products~~	~~Only uses XYZ products~~
Differentiator	We are a boutique firm that can offer customized products with exceptional customer service	Can serve multiple locations in the region	Can serve multiple locations

7.1 Differentiation Matrix

In the matrix above, I've listed "my company" as well two competitors on the top, and to the side, four key messages each firm uses to describe their expertise and how they perform the services they offer. As you can see, I've crossed out the messages from each firm that sound similar in order to find out how I can best differentiate my firm on this project. Although Competitor A and Competitor B have similar years of experience and multiple locations, I've discovered that my customized approach is a good way to differentiate myself from my competitors.

7

SUMMARY

Knowing how to set yourself apart in a positive way is critical to creating a winning proposal response. If you're not sure that you can offer something better than your competitors, then it's best not to submit a proposal until you've done more discovery or created a way that you can add more value for your prospective client or agency. In this chapter you learned:

- If you're ready to begin pursuing government work or if you still have a little more work to do;
- How to get to know a government agency better; and
- Creating differentiators to set your team apart from the competition.

In the next chapter, I'm going to walk you through a typical proposal process for a government agency or municipality.

8

PURSUING GOVERNMENT PROJECTS

 What you get by achieving your goals is not as important as what you become by achieving your goals."

Zig Ziglar

Pursuing Public Projects

If your firm has been working with public agencies, then the good news is most of the work in this chapter may have been started for you. If your firm hasn't done work in the public sector, but is interested in pursuing this type of work, I can walk you through a simple approach: 1) Be strategic; 2) Start close to home; and 3) Apply for Any small, woman-, or minority-owned business certifications for which you are eligible.

Proposal Development Phases

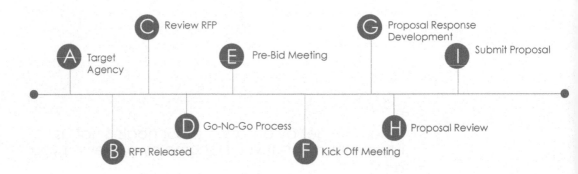

8.1 Proposal Development Matrix

It Pays to Be Strategic

Most government agencies are fairly large institutions that have strict laws governing how they can do business with the public. You may hear a lot of people talking about how much money your firm can earn through contracting with a government agency or how easy it is to get a lot of government RFPs to chase. Just because you can access a lot of RFPs doesn't mean that you should be pursuing them, since pursuing government work is very expensive. By targeting the right agencies, you can spend your time chasing work you have a high likelihood of winning instead of spreading yourself too thin and not winning much of anything.

The most important thing to realize is that, like any organization, government agencies are run by people. Although government agencies each have their share of bureaucracy and procedure, working with government agencies is no different than working with and winning over private companies. Make sure that you meet with procurement staff and department heads. Begin to build a professional working relationship with someone inside the organization who knows your firm and can advocate on your behalf when you go after your next project. Also, remember that a lot of firms are probably going after the same project you are. If you have a good relationship coupled with a fantastic RFP response, you'll have a much stronger chance of winning a project than a firm that has a great proposal response but no relationship within the agency.

Start Close to Home
Before you spend any money on lead generation or tools that help you access thousands of RFPs, start close to home. If your company is located in Tampa, Florida, then start with the City of Tampa, the county that surrounds it (Hillsborough), the local school district, and any public universities. When you win an opportunity with one of the local agencies or institutions closest to you, then it's time to expand your circle a little further. However, I would strongly advise you that when you're first starting out, it makes the best sense to stick close to home. Get to know those agencies and the department heads, and then work your circle out once you have a few project wins under your belt.

When you've identified a few of the agencies and institutions closest to home, start setting appointments to meet with the procurement department and the department heads. For example, if you sell computer equipment, you will first want to meet with the procurement department of the agency or institution you're interested in to find out more about their specific procurement process. Next, you'll want to see if the procurement person can refer you to the department head who would help make the buying decision for any computer equipment. Once you've met with those two departments, you'll probably have a better idea of what projects or contracts may be coming out in the next 12-18 months.

It Pays to Be a Small, Woman-, or Minority-Owned Business
If you work for a small firm, you may qualify locally and federally as a small or disadvantaged business. For most city, county, and public institutions, you can submit a little paperwork and become qualified as a small, woman-, or minority-owned business. These types of certifications are very useful for certain types of contracts. Doing work with the government is a process. You want to make sure that any time you spend is directed in activities that can win you work.

Develop Strategic Partnerships

If your firm is too large or doesn't qualify as a small, woman-, or minority-owned business, just make sure that you start to form relationships with these types of businesses that could possibly serve as subcontractors for your firm on a project. If you don't know who some of these partners might be, each government agency's procurement department usually has a list they are willing to share with larger vendors interested in doing business with the agency.

Finding RFPs

After you've targeted the best agencies and institutions for your firm, you have a variety of ways to check in and see what opportunities available. In this section, I'll give you an overview of a few ways you can find government RFPs and opportunities to bid on.

The Agency's Website

For a while, Onvia had a majority of the business for publishing government bids (more about that later). Unfortunately, that service started to get too expensive for most small and medium-sized businesses. So, some agencies started either posting opportunities on their own respective procurement websites, or worse, creating their own procurement and bid systems. The main reason you need to target a few agencies from the beginning and learn their systems is because it can be time-consuming getting set up with each agency based on their procurement process. If you target those agencies that you have the best shot at winning with, you'll spend less time subscribing, applying, and reviewing opportunities that you may have no shot at winning. Government agencies will always meet with you and encourage you to bid (they want to maintain a competitive marketplace). What they won't do is tell you that you're wasting your time until you realize for yourself that it's too late and you've already done so. Focus on no more than three to six agencies until you get your first win.

Onvia DemandStar

If you're doing a quick scan once or twice a week looking at your three key government agencies, then you might want to go to a source like DemandStar (https:// www.demandstar.com/). DemandStar is a government subscription service that has pretty much every agency you'll need (City, County, K-12, State, and Federal) but not all private and public universities. When you first start out and are targeting just a few agencies, you can use DemandStar for free. If you want to download an RFP, it will cost you $5. If your firm is new to government procurement, I recommend sticking with the free option until you win your first opportunity.

Shifting from Free to Paid Subscriptions

Once you've made a profit from your first government contract then, you can go and spend a little money on a subscription to Onvia that will give you a larger amount of RFPs from city, state, and federal agencies or a subscription-based service of your choice. But I would highly recommend only targeting a few agencies, establishing a reputation with those agencies, and then moving on to others.

The most comprehensive subscription service you can get for government bids is Onvia, although there are many other services out there. If you're in IT, business consulting, offer legal services, or marketing services, Onvia is your best bet. If you're in the A/E/C industry, IMS (http://www.imsinfo.com/) is a great service to try as well and is less expensive than Onvia.

More Bids Doesn't Necessarily Equal More Wins

Although it's true, you can't hit the ball if you don't take a swing, when it comes to government contracts, you can lose a lot of money and a lot of time if you're not strategic in what you're chasing and submit bids on projects and services you're not qualified to complete. In the Go-No-Go section, I'll talk more about making sure you target the right opportunities so you don't waste your company's resources.

Once the RFP is Released

After tracking one to three government agencies or institutions, you'll see an opportunity that looks pretty good at first glance. In this section, we'll walk through what a "Cone of Silence" is, a process to review the RFP, and how to "go-no-go" an opportunity. If you've done a great job with the pre-sell process as outlined in Chapter 4, then you are prepared for the RFP.

Remember the Cone of Silence

Once a RFP is released, you're typically not allowed to reach out to a selection committee or the department heads – this is known as the "cone of silence." You're only allowed to contact the procurement professional and ask them questions. However, every agency is different and hopefully you learned more about the agency's preferences during the pre-sell process.

How to Review the RFP

Most RFPs are written over a period of time and have a lot of hands involved in the process. With that said, when you review an RFP, you'll find a lot of contradictions and errors. The best way to approach the review of an RFP is my three-step process.

Step 1 - Read and Highlight Key Requirements and Dates

Print, read, and highlight key requirements and dates in the RFP. By the time you are done with this process, your RFP document should be multiple colors, contained tabbed portions, and multiple folded pages. In its book, "Writing Business Bids and Proposal for Dummies," the Association of Proposal Management Professionals (APMP) uses the metaphor "shredding" to describe the process for reviewing an RFP: "Shredding is an appropriate metaphor because you chop up the proposal - question by question, line by line, word by word - until you have a listing of every need, every want, and every wish you can find."

Skimming through a .PDF version of an RFP is okay out of necessity, but it's more effective to have a hard copy to mark up. You just see things differently in print.

During this first read-through, grab a highlighter and start highlighting important information such as:

- Procurement Specialist Name and Contact Information
- Date of the pre-bid conference (depending on the size of the project, there may not be a pre-bid conference)
- Date questions to the agency are due
- Forms - Which forms are required and do you have enough time to complete?
- Long-lead items from third parties - Is a performance bond or insurance documentation required? Make sure you make a note.
- Scope of work - Mark items that may be beyond your current abilities. Perhaps you might need to team with someone.
- SBE / WBE / MBE - Note any disadvantaged business requirements. If your firm qualifies for a designation, you should have begun the process prior to the RFP being released or you should have worked on building relationships with other firms who qualify so you can use them as sub-consultants for your proposal.

Step 2 - Highlight Unclear Items

Now that you've read the RFP, go back and read it again. This time, look for terms you don't understand, or contradictory statements given in the RFP. Highlight these items in a different color. Usually, these are the items that are good questions to ask at the pre- bid conference or items to submit to the procurement specialist responsible for the administration of the RFP process.

Step 3 - Make a List

Develop a list of all the items you found in Step 2 (could be called a proposal check list or compliance check list). You want to take this list with you to the pre-bid meeting or submit these questions to the procurement specialist. Make sure that you double check the RFP to see if a question you plan on asking wasn't already covered in the RFP. It's a little embarrassing when you submit a question, and the agency issues an addendum with your question and notes the page and paragraph where the answer to your question is written.

After you've done a thorough review of the RFP, it's time to have a Go-No-Go meeting with key staff. I'll talk more about the Go-No-Go process in the next section.

Go-No-Go Process

Now that you've thoroughly reviewed the RFP and have a more complete understanding of what the client is looking for, you need to have a go-no-go meeting to decide if the opportunity is one your firm will decide to pursue. Most go-no-go meetings are attended by key staff from operations, marketing, and business development. Before completing the Questionnaire below, it is important that each member of your team has read the RFP (especially the scope of work).

A word of advice from Carol Scheafnocker, an A/E/C industry veteran, in regards to going after proposals you haven't heard of before seeing the RFP released: "Remember that if you are seeing the RFP and that is the first time you know about the project, there is a 99% chance you will not get it. Other firms have done their homework and set themselves up to win. You must have an advocate for your firm on the selection committee, or you will not win."

Cost To Pursue

As you go through the Go-No-Go Questionnaire, your team needs to consider whether or not the agency's budget for the project makes it worth while to pursue the opportunity. If the budget for the project is not large enough for your firm to obtain a high enough fee to cover all of the time and effort going after the opportunity, the return on investment (ROI) may not be high enough to pursue the opportunity in the first place.

If you've determined the project budget is large enough, begin completing the Go-No-Go Questionnaire given below to help you determine if the opportunity is a match for your current level of expertise. If you'd like a digital copy, please go to www.chazrossmunro.com.

Go-No-Go Questionnaire

Go-No-Go Questionnaire

1. **We met with the procurement department before the RFP came out.**
   YES (1 Point)   NO (0 Points)
2. **We met with the department heads before the RFP came out (six months prior).**
   YES (1 Point)   NO (0 Points)
3. **We have a GREAT relationship with someone on the selection committee.**
   YES (2 Points) NO (0 Points)
4. **We have done three to five projects or provided services in the past three to five years exactly like the project or service outlined in the scope of work.**
   YES (1 Point)   NO (0 Points)
5. **We can perform 80% of the services outlined in the scope of work and if we have to outsource, we have an established track record with the consultants we would outsource selected services to.**
   YES (1 Point)   NO (0 Points)
6. **We have successfully completed three to five projects or provided services exactly like the project or service outlined in the scope of work for A SIMILAR CONTRACT VALUE.**
   YES (1 Point)   NO (0 Points)
7. **We have great references for each project and service of similar scope to that specified in the RFP.**
   YES (1 Point)   NO (0 Points)
8. **We have three team members who have provided services or completed projects similar to the scope of work within the last three to five years and have a track record of working on projects together.**
   YES (1 Point)   NO (0 Points)
9. **We were profitable completing projects and services similar to the scope of work specified in the RFP within the last three to five years or have a great ROI on projects of similar scope.**
   YES (1 Point)   NO (0 Points)

It's a Go
If you scored eight points or higher, then you definitely want to go to the pre-bid conference (if there is one) and/or start working on your RFP response submittal.

Need More Information
If you scored six or seven points on the go-no-go form, then you should go to the Pre-Bid Conference or ask a few clarifying questions to the procurement specialist to see if that might help you score the go-no-go a little higher.

It's a No Go
If you scored five points or less, it's probably a "no-go" proposal and it's best not to go after this project. Based on the areas you were weak on, you may want to schedule a meeting with the department heads AFTER the proposal process for the specific project is over. Get clarification and more information on how you can position your firm to be more competitive for the next bid.

Pre-Bid Conference
When you attend an agency's pre-bid conference, it will be attended by consultants and sub-consultants looking to team up with consultants who would like to be prime contractors for the bid. It's always interesting to observe how different companies approach the pre-bid conference.

When I attend pre-bid conferences, I usually try to do four things: be visible; listen to all of the information; ask questions; and pay attention to the pre-bid attendee list. Below is a little more information about each tip.

Be Visible
Usually when I attend a pre-bid conference, I try to sit towards the front. Even though the government procurement process is supposed to be non-biased, you still want to make sure you're memorable. By sitting in the front, my company and my RFP response may be a little more recognizable by the selection committee. It's a competitive market, so I'll take any advantage I can get!

Listen to All of the Information (Even the Boring Stuff)
Pre-bid meetings typically begin with a procurement manager reading key portions of the RFP and/ or pointing out which aspects will be clarified with an addendum later. This part of the meeting is pretty tedious (but necessary) and it's usually challenging to maintain one's attention as the procurement specialist goes through the procurement process for

the agency. Being read to from the RFP can take anywhere between 15–20 minutes, however, I've been in meetings where this portion of the meeting can take an hour. It's a good idea to pay attention during this part because you'll be surprised by how many important details the procurement officer points out that you may have glazed over when first reading the RFP.

Ask Questions and Listen to the Questions Asked

Following the read-through of the general procurement procedures and the proposed schedule, a project manager usually goes over the scope of work. Here's where it gets a little more exciting as more information about the project is disclosed. Questions start popping up from the attendees and you learn the key concerns for the agency. This information is critical for your RFP response. Pay attention! Make sure you incorporate these aspects into the narrative of your proposal – especially in the cover letter.

Pay Attention to the Pre-bid Attendee List

Following the pre-bid meeting, you can usually get a copy of the attendees from Demandstar, the agency will email them to you, or the agency's procurement site. The pre-bid list is extremely useful because you can get a feel for who your competition is for the contract.

Kickoff Meeting

If you are pulling a team together for an RFP pursuit, it's a good idea to have a kickoff meeting to outline expectations and deliverables. This will ensure a great proposal in less time and hopefully less pain. The best way to avoid a mad dash to the deadline is to have a kickoff meeting immediately after the pre-bid meeting.

Meeting Preparation

Only invite key staff members to the kickoff meeting. Usually the principal, project manager, marketing coordinator, and business development manager are involved in these meetings. When setting up the meeting with your team, make sure you tell everyone in your calendar invite to read the RFP before the meeting. It doesn't hurt to attach a copy of the original RFQ or RFP from the client so there are no excuses for not reading it.

Proposal Plan

The best way to prepare for a kick-off meeting is to prepare a Proposal Response Plan. The Proposal Plan can also serve as a checklist before you submit your proposal. Here's how you do it:

1. Pick your favorite tool (Word or Excel).
2. Create a proposal outline in a table format based on the structure the RFP provides. For example: Section 1 - Understanding of Services and Approach; and Section 2 - Qualifications
3. Add three columns labeled: "Notes," "Responsible," and "Deadline."
4. Create space for the team.
5. Create space for relevant project experience.
6. Proposed Schedule: Draft 1 will be completed on this date, Draft 2 will be created on this date.
7. List general proposal requirements (12-point font, double-sided, 50-page limit, number of copies, etc.)
8. List proposal delivery requirements (time, place, etc.). Don't forget to list a space for addenda and who will be checking for them.
9. Additional Questions to ask the procurement specialist.

Experience and Capacity: The offeror shall provide the following:		Notes
1	Provide the legal name and address of the qualified and registered professional.	Cover Letter
2	A summary of the offeror's experience lobbying before the executive and legislative branches in Florida.	Resumes and Project Sheets
3	Provide evidence to demonstrate credible and positive working relationships with members of the legislature and executive branch, their staff and state agencies - particularly those with jurisdiction over general issues facing local governments in Florida. Evidence must also be provided that demonstrates familiarity with members of the legislature, their offices, their staff, local delegations, their staff, and relevant committee (appropriations and authorizations) chairs, and their staffs.	How to demonstrate this?
4	Provide previous work examples that demonstrate the ability to effectively position the County to achieve funding and other goals related to local government issues and improvements. Provide evidence, if any, to demonstrate other valuable resources such as strategic alliances, partnerships, or relationships that would support you (your firm) in advancing the County's interests.	Project Sheets - could go into more detail on strategic alliances and partnerships (if applicable)
5	The offeror's disclosure of any potential conflict of interest due to any other clients, contracts, or property interests. Include statement certifying that no member of your firm's ownership, management, or staff has a vested interest in any aspect of, or department under the Pasco County Board of County Commissioners.	Do you have a blanket policy?
References & Successes		
1	Provide a client list for the past five (5) to seven (7) years. The client list shall include the following:	
	Client's or organziation's name	Project Sheets
	Contact name(s), title(s), address(es) and telephone number(s) for each client.	Project Sheets
	Duration of relationship	Project Sheets
	Type of service provided (including the area of legislative interest).	Project Sheets - could go into more detail on specific legislators, executive officers or agency heads.
	Primary legislators, executive officers, or agency heads associated with each client listed.	Project Sheets
2	Provide a summary of all successful lobying efforts for the past (5) to seven (7) years. Each summary shall include:	Project Sheets and Experience Overviews
	A brief summary of the problem (background).	Project Sheets
	A brief summary of the work process (methodology).	Project Sheets
	A brief summary of the solution (success).	Project Sheets - could go into more detail on project successes.
Methodology & Pricing		
1	A concise statement why the County should select your firm as its lobbyist for the specified issues.	Cover Letter
2	The offeror shall provide a fee schedule for the services specified in this request.	How do you charge?

8.01 Proposal Plan

Don't Leave Until You Have the Answers

Do not leave the kickoff meeting until you have every item on your proposal plan taken care of, someone responsible for giving you the information, and a date and time when the task will be completed. In some cases, you may be in charge of most of the items, but the main point of this exercise is accountability.

Follow Up

When the deadlines approach, start following up with team members and remind them, "This is what we agreed to at the kickoff meeting, do you have item 2 ready?"

Information Organization and Management

Organizing your proposal information is important to make sure you don't miss key details and stay on top of all the information you'll manage as you complete your proposal response. I typically have the format demonstrated below saved and that way I can just cut and paste whenever I have a new proposal project. In this section, I'll walk you through my proposal organizational system.

01 Original RFP

02 Project Management

03 Research & Rough Drafts

04 Graphics

05 Working Docs

06 Drafts for Review

07 Printer

08 Final and Proof of Delivery

09 Shortlist Presentation

10 Debrief

8.2 Proposal Information File Structure

Limit Access

I find it's best to have one person responsible for managing all of the proposal information and placing it in the correct folder. If you decide to use Dropbox, Google Docs, or another type of shared file system, make sure the proposal coordinator (or the person responsible for pulling the entire document together) is placing the content in each file. The only file a proposal team should share is the "Research & Rough Drafts" file. In a tight deadline with multiple files changing and too many hands involved, I've seen files go missing or people editing the wrong files. The proposal coordinator should manage all of the documents, oversee version control, and be the only one touching the master proposal documents.

01 Original RFP
In the "Original RFP" file, I keep all of the original RFP documents including addenda and documents from the agency or client. I usually always have a printed and marked up copy on my desk at all times, but I also like having this file at the top in case anyone needs a copy.

02 Project Management
I use the "Project Management" file for any administrative and project management functions related to the proposal. If I'm working with a big team for a proposal, I'll have a list of all the subcontractors we're using and their information. I also keep the proposal plan in this file.

03 Research & Rough Drafts
The "Research & Rough Drafts" folder is self-explanatory. I like having a file where I can put my drafts and keep it separate from some of the other proposal documents I track.

04 Graphics
Whether it's screen shots of applications your firm has developed or marked-up site plans, it's a good idea to have one folder for all of these materials. A lot of times you'll use graphics from previous proposals so it's always nice if you can go to one folder to dig up a .JPEG you need instead of having to go through the entire proposal document.

05 InDesign Working Docs
I use InDesign for all of my proposal documents, but many organizations use Microsoft Word documents as well. I've even seen some proposals produced on PowerPoint slides. I like keeping the main working documents out of the other files in case I need to share documents with other members of my team. If I'm sharing my files on Dropbox, I'll usually share the "Research & Rough Drafts" file with the team but I never share my "Working Docs" file because I don't want anyone to accidentally delete something. Remember to save all versions of the working drafts. You never know when someone will want to go back to a previous draft and work something back into the narrative that was taken out previously.

06 Drafts
The "Drafts" file is for all .PDF or marked-up drafts I either send to the team

or receive from the team as mark-ups.

07 Printer
The "Printer" file is for the materials I send to the printer, which usually includes covers and tabs.

08 Final and Proof of Delivery
The "Final and Proof of Delivery" file is the final compiled draft of the entire proposal. In this file, I also save the proof of delivery. If I mail the proposal, I get the email proof of receipt and save it in this file. If I deliver the proposal in person, I take a picture of the proof of receipt slip and save it in this file.

09 Shortlist Presentation
If my team is shortlisted for the project, I save all of the presentation preparation materials in this folder.

10 Debrief
Win or lose, it's always a great idea to debrief. After the debrief, I place my notes and score sheets in the "Debrief" folder.

First Things First
After the kickoff meeting, there are several things to address on your proposal response. These items don't take a lot of time and getting them done right off the bat can help get you started on your entire proposal.

Client Past Performance Surveys
If your proposal contains past performance surveys or reference request forms as part of the RFP requirements, then make sure you start on these forms as soon as possible! Your clients are typically busy and it is not a priority for your past clients to respond to these types of documents. Therefore, it may take a little more reminding and follow-up to make sure your past clients complete these forms on time. You can get marked as "non-compliant" if your client doesn't complete these forms in a timely fashion. The bottom line is: you need to make this process as easy as possible for your client to complete. If your client has to look for any of the information, you may jeopardize winning the project for a non-compliant proposal. If your RFP contains these types of forms, make sure you do the following to get them turned in on time:
1. Give your client everything they'll need. If the forms need to be submitted by mail back to the agency, make sure you send the forms and an envelope with the correct mailing address to the client. Depending on your timeline and where your client is, you may need to overnight the forms or deliver the forms in person.
2. Call to verify. If the forms can be submitted electronically, make sure you send the forms by email and then make sure you contact the client to verify receipt.
3. Pre-fill it out. Depending on your relationship with the client, you may want to fill in

information or provide the information separately for the client

Notify Subject Matter Experts and Sub-consultants about Content

When you did your proposal plan for the kickoff meeting, you may have discovered a few items that require Subject Matter Experts (SMEs) and sub-consultants to write content for. Now is a good time to email and call these SMEs with copies of the questions they need to respond to, the format for responding, and the deadline by when you need the information.

Covers, Tabs, and Packaging

As soon as you have a "go" for a proposal, begin designing and printing your proposal covers and tabs. Covers and tabs won't change really from the start of your draft through to the completion. If your firm has brand standards, your covers and tabs will need some modifications but will be a standard template you can modify easily. Go ahead and get these items printed first. I recommend sending your covers and tabs to the printer right after the kickoff meeting. Shortly after I send covers and tabs to the printer, I'll also work on the sticker or any labeling I'll need for the box to deliver the proposal. Printing these items ahead of time can really save you a headache on the day a proposal is due.

Start with the Easiest Items First

After you've sent out your past performance surveys (if required), created your covers, tabs, and packaging, it's now time to turn your attention to the proposal itself. After completing your proposal plan, you likely discovered a few items you can take care of right away. Start working on these components and try to knock out as many as you can as early as possible in your proposal completion process. If you start with some of the more complex narrative, you may get stuck and not accomplish all of the little requirements you already have information for. By starting with the easiest tasks first, you won't miss out on an opportunity due to overlooking a small detail.

Cover Letter

Cover letters are one of the most important documents you'll write and include in your proposals, although they are often an afterthought to most proposal submittals. A cover letter is the first impression of your proposal. You may remember from the etiquette chapter how important your first impression presentation can be.

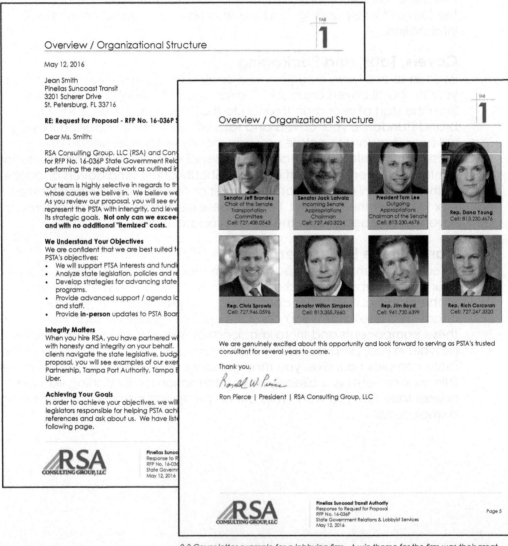

8.3 Cover letter example for a lobbying firm. A win theme for the firm was their great reputation with key government officials. To emphasize the win theme, images of key officials were used on the 2nd page of the cover letter.

Differentiators and Win Themes

If you've ever gone to a play or participated in theatre, you know that people don't show up to watch a play so they can listen to actors read the lines. They show up to see the subtext. Audiences are interested in how the lines are said and the actors' choices when delivering these lines. When you write a cover letter, you're trying to give more subtext to the overall proposal. Your client understands their own challenges on the project and what the project basically entails, but how are you going to deliver a solution to your client in a way that sets you apart from your competitors? A win theme is developed from your differentiators. Great cover letters introduce a win theme in the cover letter and then carry it out through the rest the proposal.

Keep It Short and Sweet

RFPs often include a laundry list of requirements to submit. The cover letter is your opportunity to shine and to spotlight key areas of concern the client may have brought up during the project discovery period. However, you need to do all of this in one page. Trying to summarize all of the key elements of what your company can bring to a project in one page is by no means easy. As Mark Twain said, "I didn't have time to write a short letter, so I wrote a long one instead." Perhaps this explains why most marketing and business development professionals put off writing the cover letter to the very end – it's one of the more challenging elements to write in a proposal despite being one of the shortest.

With that said, here's a basic format you can borrow to write your cover letter:
1. Thank the client for the opportunity to submit.
2. Summarize the problem the client is facing and your solution.
3. Win themes or three supporting reasons your firm is the best to solve the problem.
4. Close the letter by restating your desire to work with the client.

Repeating Your Win Theme Throughout the Proposal

After you delineate your differentiators and win theme in your cover letter, make sure you continue to reiterate them throughout the rest of your proposal. Often, selection committees review certain components of your proposal based on their expertise and may choose to neglect others. If you are consistent and point out your key differentiators throughout your proposal, it will help your proposal stand out from your competitors no matter which selection committee member is reading it.

Executive Summary

Wait, don't start writing it yet! The first thing you should know about writing an executive summary is not to start writing it until you have a solid understanding of what solution you are providing for your prospective client. The purpose of an executive summary is to convince your prospective customer in one to three pages that he or she needs to buy your solution, so it's actually not a summary. As Tom Sant says in his book, "Persuasive Business Proposals," "The executive summary is the single most important part of your proposal. Its' the only part that's likely to be read by everybody involved in making a decision."

What Should Go in an Executive Summary?

1. **A summary of the problem.** What is the problem you are trying to solve for your client? What is your client concerned about? What is keeping them up at night? The main pain point for your client must be woven into the narrative of the executive summary. "We understand the challenges of creating and maintaining 50 independent websites…""Our first priority is to keep your students safe while we are constructing the new 250,000 SF facility…" "After our initial analysis, we see that your company is losing approximately $2 million a year due to…"

2. **Your solution.** Present your solution as simply as possible and avoid jargon or acronyms unless these are commonly understood by your reader. "Our solution will grow sales by more than 50%…" "Our solution will offer you the flexibility you seek for a price that is 25% less than…" "We can help your firm reduce waste by 25% by…"

3. **The benefits of your solution.** Help your potential client understand why your solution is better than your competitors. Elaborate on three to five of the benefits your solution provides and present concise evidence on how each benefit eliminates a pain point for your customer.

4. **Ask for the sale.** It is important that your potential client knows how important this opportunity is to you and your company. Depending on the type of client, you may want to interject an emotional appeal as to why you are passionate about your prospective client's project.

There are several schools of thought on how to write a great executive summary, but the best executive summaries usually start on a white board with your team outlining why your solution is the best for your potential client. Write the executive summary first and then make sure the rest of your proposal and RFP response clearly articulates and demonstrates why your solution is the best fit for your client.

How to Answer RFP Questions

It seems simple, right? Just answer the question asked in the RFP! However, you'd be surprised by how many firms struggle with this. Busy proposal writers often take some boilerplate (or standard marketing collateral) and try to force it into an answer. This isn't a good strategy. In this section, I'll give you a couple of suggestions for answering RFP questions.

It's Okay to Say Yes or No

Sometimes, a RFP question can be answered with a "yes" or "no" response. It's okay to just answer with a short response and then offer clarification. For example:

- No. XYZ is not part of our standard solution, but we can add it for $500.
- Yes. Our XYZ solution is compliant with your connectivity requirements.

Complex Questions

When you have a more complex RFP question, make sure you follow this three-step process:

1. Answer or summarize your response in the first sentence.
2. Offer clarification, proof, or examples.
3. Summarize the benefits of this approach or feature of your solution.

For example:

- XYZ solution can offer you a 25% improvement in productivity (Step 1). We've implemented more than 300 systems and all of our clients have experienced better connectivity (Step 2). 80% of our clients had improved efficiency of 40% or greater (Step 2). When ABC Company implements our solution, the increase in employee productivity will translate to increased revenues between 5-7% (Step 3).

Writer's Block

It happens to everyone: writer's block. When you get stuck in your writing process, here are a few suggestions for making progress even in your stickiest moments:

1. Skip to another section in your proposal. You don't have to work on the RFP in a linear fashion.
2. Answer the easiest questions first. If you know one section is going to be more challenging than the rest, start with the easier sections and then go back to the more challenging sections later. Sometimes answering the easiest questions can get the creative juices flowing and help you figure out how to respond to the more challenging sections.
3. Move away from the computer! Grab a piece of paper and start sketching out a response, or use a mind map. Don't let technology

stand in the way of you tapping into your creativity.

Budget
As crazy as it may sound, sometimes government agencies are not concerned with how much money you can save them. If you are working on a project that has funding allocated for two years, then the project may take the entire two years even if your firm can do it faster. That's why it's so important you take the time to get to know the department heads during the business development/project qualification process so you can determine if the overall goals for the project are a good fit for your firm as well. If the delay in funding is going to be too hard for your company to absorb for two years, then you may want to look at a different project. Another concern with budget could be excess profits. In the eyes of some agencies, excess profit is just as troublesome as deficient budgets. If there is too much money left over, then the agency starts to question whether they could have gotten more for their money. So be careful to ensure you understand what the goals for the project are. After you understand the budget goals for the project, make sure you convey this information to the project manager who is doing the overall estimate for the project.

Budget or Pricing Forms Format
If you are given forms in the original RFP, make sure you use that format in your RFP response. Even if you completely disagree with how the agency is asking for the information, submit the information EXACTLY how the agency asks for it in the RFP.

FEE SCHEDULE

DESCRIPTION	Unit	Quantity	TOTAL ANNUAL FIXED FEE (includes all expenses)
STATE LEGISLATIVE SERVICES	Annual	1	$

*NOTE: PTB does not pay separate reimbursable expenses, except as may be specifically authorized (in writing) by the Project Manager on special assignments.

HOURLY FEES / EXPENSES FOR OPTIONAL AUTHORIZED WORK
(may NOT leave this section blank)

PERSONNEL NAME / CLASSIFICATION	HOURLY RATE
	$
	$
	$
	$
	$
	$
	$
	$

Note: Must include personnel name/classification and hourly rate for all team members

By: _____   _____
                 Signature   Printed Name

_____   _____
           Name of Company   Title

                                                          _____
                                                                       Date

8.4 Example of a Pricing Form

Project Schedule or Plan

Depending on where the agency is in their process and the project, your project schedule or project plan may need to be somewhat vague or very detailed. If you sell cleaning services, then you may be wondering if you need to include a project schedule: yes. No matter what service you sell, if you can give a schedule for services, it's helpful in a proposal. Schedules show that you have a process and you know how long it takes to complete the various tasks or services your firm provides.

The goal in a proposal is to clarify things that can be ambiguous. For example, your firm may offer exceptional cleaning services and you may charge more than your competitors. In your project schedule, you may want to show how your firm spends four hours per site visit instead of the two your competitor does. Document how you complete 25 tasks in that four-hour period. If your firm is selling a professional service, you may hear that it's "too expensive," from clients. This may or may not be true. When you can give definitive examples of why your service exceeds your competitors, it becomes clear why your service should be more expensive. A project schedule or project plan is a great way to illustrate your firm's value by clarifying expectations and demonstrating you have a clear time table for completing your services.

Formatting

Robin Matson, Vice President for George F. Young, is a big advocate of presenting oneself well and she's been doing so for more than 20 years. And she's right, it makes a difference. How your present your work in your firm's RFP response is just as important as what you say.

If the RFP asks for information in a very specific way and you don't respond in kind, it shows you're not listening to the client (and that's before the project even gets started). If you've done a lot of the proposal preparation ahead of time, formatting becomes a minor issue. However, if you're having to go and hunt for a lot of the proposal information and then start formatting for the proposal, you're already behind.

Perhaps one of the most useful tools in formatting your proposals is using tables. If you're formatting a Word document and you want items to line up, use tables throughout and just remove the lines after (below).

You want to make sure that the selection committee can easily find the information.

Scope of Services

TAB

2

Tab Two - Scope of Services
- The proposal should include a full description of the requested services and methodology of provding the requested service. In addition, state how your company will meet or exceed PSTA's requirements for the requested services.
- A definitive Scope of Services based on the information contained in this RFP. Explain in detail the Consultant's approach and proposed methodology for achieving the stated objectives. Provide any foreseeable difficulties in completing the requirements of this RFP, along with a plan for resolution, or if apporopriate, propose an alternative approach.
- Select one major law, bill, etc. that has potential impact on local transit and explain your lobbying approach that would prove successful for PSTA.

The following table identifies RSA's strengths in achieving each Scope of Work item as outlined in pages 8 - 10 of RFP No. 16-036P for State Government Relations and Lobbyist Services. Following the table, several report examples have been given to illustrate the level of detail and support RSA provides each of its clients.

2.2 Scope of Work	Meet	Exceed	Additional Information
2.2.A. Maintain knowledge of issues concerning PSTA, capital, and operating needs and be prepared to offer advice and advocacy support.	✓		
2.2.B. Review and analyze, on a continuing basis, all existing and proposed State polices, programs, regulations that may impact PSTA. Provide prompt notification to PSTA of the issue and specific impact, and possible resolutions.		✓	RSA publishes a weekly newsletter that keeps all of its clients apprised on state policies, programs, and regulations that may impact RSA. Please see the "RSA Weekly Newsletter" example on pages 25-26.
2.2.C. Having strong professional relationships with Tampa Bay Delegation and State Transportation and Transportation Appropriations Leaderships.		✓	RSA has relationships with Sen. Jeff Brandes, Sen. Jack Latvala, Pres. Tom Lee, Rep. Greg Steube, Rep. Jim Boyd, Speaker-Designate Richard Corcoran; and Rep. Dana Young.
2.2.D. On issues where State and Federal Policy overlap, coordinate and collaborate with PSTA's contracted Federal lobbyist as necessary.		✓	RSA is currently working with a federal lobbyist for the Tampa Port Authority. Please see the "RSA End of Session Report" on pages 22-24.
2.2.E. Advise PSTA about funding opportunities to help delivery PSTA's programs and high priority projects.		✓	RSA has experience in advising its clients about funding opportunies. Please see examples in "Tab 3: References" section of our proposal.
2.2.F. Work with PSTA to build upon existing relationships within State agencies and to provide input on upcoming grant opportunities.	✓		
2.2.G. Assist in the development for advancing actions at the State level that are beneficial to PSTA, including drafting legislation, and sponsorship of State bills/amendments needed to further PSTA's goals and priorities.		✓	RSA will attend every meeting necessary to ensure PSTA is represented and has the opportunity to advance actions that are beneficial to PSTA on a state level.
2.2.H. Advocate PSTA's positions and priorities to the Governor's office, the Florida Legislature, and legislative branch officials.	✓		

Pinellas Suncoast Transit Authority
Response to Request for Proposal
RFP No. 16-036P
State Government Relations & Lobbyist Services
May 12, 2016

Page 19

8.5 Formatted RFP Response Document

Electronic Submittals

Many government agencies and large private companies are moving to electronic RFP systems. Although these require less formatting skills, you still need to be careful when submitting responses that use these systems. Electronic submittals can take some pain out of the proposal process, but I've also heard horror stories of people missing deadlines and losing all of their data because of system glitches. In this section, I'm going to give you a few simple steps for creating and submitting your electronic RFP responses so you don't have any problems with this type of procurement process.

Create a Draft Outside the System First

When your client is using an electronic submittal system for RFP responses, request the RFP into a format outside the electronic system so you can create a duplicate response document. Depending on the system, the client may provide you a copy of the information requested in the system via .PDF, you may be able to export a .PDF from the system itself, or you may have to take screenshots of each component of the bid (as in the pricing module shown below).

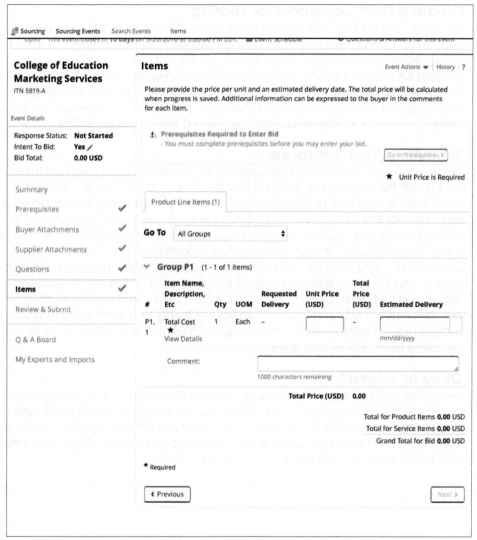

8.6 Electronic Submittal System Example

Create a Draft Document for Sharing

Next, you want to create a draft document in Excel or Word so you and your team can create responses and make edits to the answers to the RFP questions. In the Excel draft document example below, there is a column for each question, answer, and the character count. Your format may need to change based on the type of system your client is using. The most important factor is having a sharable document that people on your team can edit and review before you submit the response online.

Submitting Your Response

Once you've created your responses and your team has reviewed them and given their approval, it's time to submit your RFP response. If possible, try to submit your response a day early. When you're trying to upload your responses at the same time as 10 other vendors, technology glitches start to happen. Spare yourself the stress and submit your proposal either a day early or many hours ahead of the actual deadline. If you submit early, chances are you'll avoid any technology issues and if something does go wrong, you still have time to contact procurement or the client represen-tative and get assistance. Both procurement and client representatives are much more willing to help when you're trying to submit early and experience a problem than when you call five minutes before or after the deadline because of problems.

Okay to Submit?

Next time you have an electronic submittal, take the time to download a complete RFP document or all of the screen shots, create a duplicate response in an Excel or Word Document, and remember to submit early so that you don't have any issues. If you follow each of these steps, your next electronic submittal will be glitch- and worry-free.

8

SUMMARY

In this chapter, you learned how to pursue government projects and a few tactics for making sure your next pursuit runs smoothly. A few important ideas to remember:

- Be strategic in the type of government opportunities you're looking for, the geographical area you should focus on, and how being a small, woman-, or minority-owned firm can help you, the next step is to find out how to access opportunities as they're available.
- Make the most out of a pre-bid conference. The next time you pursue a contract, make sure you attend the pre-bid meeting no matter how busy you may be. If you can't attend, make sure you send someone who can represent your firm.
- Stick with the process! Your team will get used to the overall process and it will make getting your content together easier.
- A key component of writing and winning a proposal is knowing how to prioritize your time so you don't lose a project on a technicality that you could have easily controlled. By reaching out to clients early for past performance surveys, soliciting assistance from SMEs and sub-consultants early, creating some of your printed materials in advance, and answering the easiest items first, you can make sure you stay on track for completing the best proposal on time.
- Write the executive summary first and then make sure the rest of your proposal and RFP response clearly articulates and demonstrates why your solution is the best fit for your client.
- Create your responses to electronic submittals in an Excel or Word document first, and then submit electronically once you have all of the information and it's been reviewed by your staff.

In the next chapter, you'll learn a few tips and tricks to make your proposals stand out from the competition.

9

HIGH-IMPACT PROPOSALS

 "Excellence is not a singular act; it's a habit. You are what you repeatedly do."

Aristotle

Great Proposals Are Focused on a Win Theme

When Steve Jobs pitched the iPod, he pitched one key idea: a device that could fit "1,000 songs in your pocket." Jobs didn't create a slide that had all of the tech specs for the product and then begin to talk about processor speed, onboard RAM, connectivity, battery type, the built-in display, or full-charge time. It didn't matter. It was 1,000 songs in your pocket!

You need to approach your proposals with the same focus Steve Jobs did while pitching his technology products. When you're selling a service, you are the product. Don't be complicated.

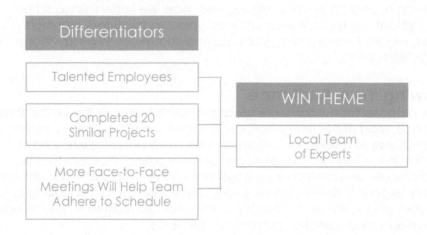

9.0 Establishing differentiators and creating a win theme.

Hopefully during your pre-sell process, you obtained more background information on the project and determined some of the key issues for the project's success that weren't outlined in the RFP. In your proposal, you show that you listened to your client by repeating these hot buttons and how you plan on solving them. Try to get these main points down to three and tie them together with a win theme. Nothing must stand in the way between your win theme connecting with your client. I promise you at least one of your competitors will not have a win theme that ties together these overused differentiators:

1. We will be on time.
2. We will be within your budget.
3. We will exceed your expectations.

Do everything you can within your power not to make one of the three items above your win theme. When I worked with a software subcontractor on a project pursuit for a municipality client, their win theme was "We're local." We learned in our discovery process that face-to-face meetings were very important to the client. We also knew from our discovery process that our competitors didn't have a strong local presence.

Throughout our proposal, we reiterated our "we're local" win theme. Once shortlisted for the project, the entire team came to the presentation. Typically it's best to limit the amount of people that participate in the presentation. However in this particular scenario, we knew some of the other consultants were using subcontractors from other parts of the world. By having a local and overwhelming presence, we knew this would be a huge advantage for us. If you can keep your proposals focused on a win theme, you will connect with your selection committee in a way that your competitors aren't.

Knowing Your Audience

Great proposal teams can write great proposals because they know their audience. Most of the time when you respond to RFPs, you are submitting your response to a selection committee that may not necessarily have expertise in the service and solution your firm is selling. It's important to communicate and craft your proposal document to speak to the different types of people reviewing your response. Typically, you are speaking to two types of audiences: the technical selection committee members and the non-technical selection committee members.

Non-Technical Selection Committee Audience

The non-technical selection committee audience consists of procurement specialists, legal representation, and finance or accounting representatives for the organization. In many cases, these professionals are brought in to oversee the procurement process and to ensure whatever solution is selected is feasible cost-wise. These selection committee members have the following concerns:

1. Is the proposal response compliant? The non-technical selection committee members are reviewing your proposal to ensure that your firm followed the instructions outlined in the RFP. Did your firm fill out all of the forms and follow the format? These members are looking for a way to throw out your proposal based on a technicality. Even if your firm did the pre-sell correctly, but you miss a section or don't submit a form in your proposal, this can be all it takes to disqualify your proposal. Usually, it's the non-technical staff that sees your proposal

first. If your response isn't compliant, your proposal will not be seen by the technical selection committee members.
2. Is the proposal response within budget? These selection committee members will usually read your cover letter (and it had better be good) and then flip directly to the cost section of your proposal. If the CFO is reading the proposal, those two components of your proposal may be the only things he or she reads.
3. Does the proposal look like the team really wants the job? Since the non- technical selection committee members don't specialize in the service your proposal is selling, they will definitely be more influenced by the graphic design elements and overall look of the proposal to see if it communicates your team is professional and really wants the project. Proposals that have tons of grammatical errors and shoddy formatting will communicate that your firm isn't serious about the project and may impact their scoring of your proposal.

Technical Selection Committee Audience

The technical selection committee audience consists of department heads or other key staff that truly understand the complexity of what you're selling. Some of these individuals may have an educational background similar to the principals of your firm.

These selection committee members usually have the following concerns:
1. Can this team do the work they say they can do? Your technical audience is going to look at your experience and determine if your experience lines up with the project at hand. They will be the best judges on whether your firm can handle the project.
2. What will this team be like to work with? Hopefully, your firm did a little pre- sell and the technical selection committee members have already been introduced to key staff on your team responsible for completing the project. This question brings to light how the selection committee wants to know that your team understands the constraints they're working under. Does your team understand how to make the selection committee member's job easier? Great proposals communicate these concerns in the project approach and in the proposal narrative when appropriate.
3. Do they really want the job? If your proposal is lacking in quality, substance, and heavy in boilerplate (or materials that are used repeatedly in proposals), it may convey that winning this project isn't really a priority for your team. Making sure your proposal is technically compliant and answers all the questions is the bare minimum for a successful proposal response. The excellent proposal responses that win work are highly customized, and answer questions in a way

that not only shows an understanding for the technical challenges, but speak to the emotional concerns of the technical selection committee members as well.

Great Proposal Features Every Reviewer Appreciates

Can you imagine reviewing 20 very technical proposals that vary in length between 50-100 pages? That means the selection committee has to read between 1,000 to 2,000 pages! Can you imagine making notes and trying to cite reasons why each proposal measures up and why it doesn't? Now you're starting to get an idea of what it's like to be a member on the selection committee. It's not an easy job. With that in mind, you need to make it as easy to read and absorb the information as possible. I've got a few suggestions for you to help your proposals look and communicate your firm's benefits better than your competitors.

1. **Be concise.** You don't have to fill up two to three pages of text even if the RFP says you have two to three pages to elaborate. If you can get your point across in a few sentences and some bullets, do it.
2. **Use headings and subheadings.** If you have to insert large blocks of narrative to properly address a question, make sure you use headings and subheadings. The selection committee will usually skim through your proposal and read sections that are of the most interest to them. I wish I could say that every section of your proposal will be read, but it probably won't. Make sure that you summarize each block of text with headings and subheadings that can help guide your readers. This also breaks up the text and makes it easier on reviewers' eyes.
3. **Use graphics.** Instead of one page of text documenting a process your firm uses, try creating a graphic that illustrates this process. Your selection committee will thank you. One word of advice about graphics: use graphics that are relevant to your proposal and to the project. Images of your staff, graphics about your process, and images of past projects are all great ideas. If you're designing a school and you insert a few pictures of students, that might work to show you understand who the end users are for the project. Using graphics that are in no way relevant to your project distract your reader from the key messaging your proposal is seeking to communicate. Don't distract your reader with imagery and graphics that won't help them understand your firm's value as a trusted consultant. Stay away from clip art!
4. **Use tables.** Another great way to limit the amount of text in your proposal while still communicating a lot of information is to use a table. You may not consider this a graphical element, but I've created some beautiful tables that illustrate information in an elegant way.
5. **Stay within the page limit.** Sometimes, page limits seem almost

unreasonable with the type of questions a client or agency may ask. Your team will probably fight you on reducing content they wrote, but if it doesn't work within the page limit requirements, you will have to cut somewhere. A good compromise might be to add an appendix in the back of your proposal with the pertinent information. Just be aware and make your team aware that the content may not be read.

Stay Focused and Stand out

The selection committee reviewing your proposal is usually reviewing several other proposals as well. In order to make your proposal stand apart from the competition, your proposal must appeal to both non-technical and technical selection committee members. Writing a great proposal response that speaks to multiple audiences is challenging. If your proposal is concise and uses graphics to illustrate complex concepts, then you're halfway there to persuading a selection committee to choose your team for its next project.

Proposal Production

Although the digital revolution has occurred, many proposals for both public and private sector clients are still printed on paper and submitted in duplicate. With that in mind, having a plan for the proposal print production is essential. Some firms don't really think about printing the proposal until the day the proposal is due. However, it is best to take a different strategy.

Outsource Covers and Tabs

Even if you have a really great printer and can print card stock and tabs in house, I recommend using a vendor. Covers and tabs are a few of the things you can outsource, so do it! The most important aspects of your proposal are the things you can't outsource. Card stock paper can tear up your printer and cause it to jam.

Do Not Print the Day the Proposal is Due

It never fails, your printer will break the day a proposal is due. Always try to print your proposal or, at a minimum, most of your content, the day before the proposal is due. If you are mailing the proposal, add a few days to your timeline for extra printing time.

You Will Find One More Mistake

As you print your proposal, you will find a mistake. I have yet to print out a "final" proposal only to discover midway through 200 pages that there is a huge mistake on page 45 that is going to add to my page count and throw off all of my page numbers - causing a reprint. Again, give yourself extra time during final production because when you print your proposal, you are going to find a few mistakes and you want to give yourself time to resolve these issues.

Don't Let the Printing Devil Get You
Printing your proposal may seem like the easiest part of the process, but you'd be surprised how many war stories I've heard of malfunctioning printers and last-minute changes causing seasoned professionals to miss deadlines. Don't let that happen to you! Print early and outsource the parts you can. It could make the difference between winning the job and missing the opportunity entirely.

Collaborating with a Team
When you work on a proposal with a team, the idea of shared documents that everyone can edit with his or her section sounds appealing. A few recommendations will ensure that the collaboration process runs smoothly.

Project Team Contact Sheet
Before the kickoff meeting, create a list of everyone on the team, his or her role, cell phone, and email address. Email the list to everyone on the team so each team member knows who is on the team and how best to reach them.

Take Time to Brainstorm
One of the best things about working on a team is getting a lot of ideas from different people. At the kickoff meeting, give your team time to talk about the client, what you've learned from the pre-sell process, and brainstorm creative ideas for approaching your prospective clients' problem(s). Many times, teams jump right into the proposal and focus on answering the questions the same way they've answered similar questions in the past. Take the opportunity to think about other ways you could address the hot buttons and key issues. You'll be surprised with what you come up with.

Use a Hybrid Approach with Shared and Non-Shared Documents
When it comes to shared documents, I recommend a hybrid approach. First drafts for each section are perfectly okay on a Google shared document. However, the final version of the proposal document should be under the control of one person and one person only. The main reason for this is voice. When you start having multiple writers in a proposal, it can start to sound like multiple writers, which isn't a good thing. You want one

proposal voice. You can get this consistent voice if you hand over control to one person who works on maintaining the consistency of the writing. You won't confuse your readers if you have this consistency throughout your proposal.

Know the Hierarchy

Make sure you know who has the last say on any proposal content conflict and get this approved at the kickoff meeting. It is very frustrating for the proposal manager reviewing the proposal and incorporating the changes to handle conflicting review comments if he or she isn't clear on the hierarchy. As I mentioned in the editing and proofing section, knowing who has final say on proposal content is very important.

Working with Multiple Sub-consultants

If you're working on a proposal with multiple sub-consultants, inviting them in for the brainstorming process is a great idea if you can keep the meeting focused on solving specific project issues. Sub-consultants have unique knowledge pertaining to specific portions of the project, and they can open team members' minds to new and innovative ideas. Use your sub-consultants!

Also, make sure that you are very clear in your requests for information. If you can send your sub-consultants a response template and examples, this can save you a lot of time when you're trying to incorporate their responses into your proposal. I've heard countless proposal managers complain that they get bad information or poorly formatted responses. If you are not specific in your requests for content, you won't get what you need. You must also specify deadlines for when you need the information. ASAP is not a deadline. Be specific! 11 a.m. on March 21 is a deadline. You can email your request, but I recommend emailing and following up with a phone call to make sure your sub-consultant received the email. When you call, your sub knows it's important.

If You're the Sub-consultant

If your firm is the sub-consultant, it's important that you pull the information for your team as quickly as possible and get it to the prime firm for the contract in the format the prime requests. Carol Scheafnocker, A/E/C 30-year marketing veteran, gives a few other tips, "Be easy to work with. Be sure to read the RFP and send licenses or pertinent information even if the marketing professional for the prime contractor did not request it. He or she may have overlooked it. Be a real team player, even if that means going to your teammate's office on assembly day to help check and pull the response together."

Collaborating to Win

Working on large complex pursuits can be really exciting. It's important to use all of the members on your team to your full advantage. Be clear in your requests for content and specific on deadlines. If you capture your entire team's insights (internal team members and sub-consultants), your team will be well on its way to a winning proposal.

Page Layouts

Creating a great proposal response entails a lot of planning and organization. Page layout grids can create a consistent layout throughout your proposal. The best way to see how grids work is to show you a few examples. In my examples, I've used a 5 x 5 grid. If you are using a program like InDesign, you can create an invisible grid guide in your document. If you are using Word, you can either create a table and remove the lines later or just keep the ratios in mind as you place your graphics and verbiage. On the following pages, you'll see how versatile a 5 x 5 grid can be. If you go to www.chazrossmunro.com, I've uploaded a few templates and videos to help you learn how to design a cover using a grid.

Proposal Covers

In the examples below, I've shown you how you can use a 5 x 5 grid to create a great cover page layout.

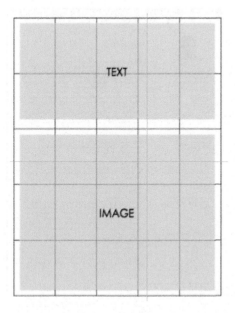

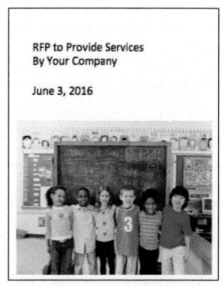

9.1 Cover option A designed with 5 x 5 grid.

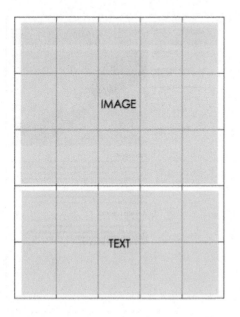

9.2 Cover option B designed with 5 x 5 grid.

Resume and Project Sheet Pages

Here is an example of resume and project sheet grids with actual resumes and project sheets.

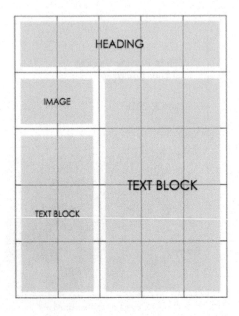

9.3 *Resume designed with 5 x 5 grid.*

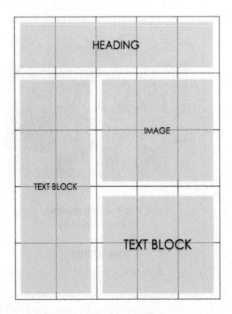

9.4 *Project sheet designed with 5 x 5 grid.*

Proposal Response Pages

Here is an example of formatted proposal response pages with the use of 5 x 5 grid templates.

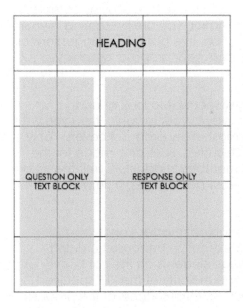

9.5 Proposal response A on 5 x 5 grid template.

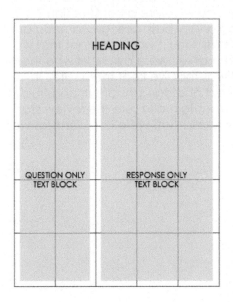

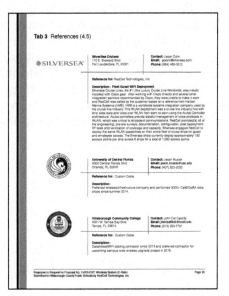

9.6 Proposal response B on 5 x 5 grid template.

Graphics

If you have great graphics in your proposals, your readers and reviewers will thank you. Instead of giving your readers pages of text to read, create tables, charts, images, or other graphics to make it as easy as possible for your audience to understand the information you are presenting in your proposals. Before you start inserting clip art, I've got a few suggestions on how to get the most bang for your buck in your proposal graphics.

Keep It Simple

If it takes your reader longer than a few seconds to look at and understand what you are trying to convey in your graphic, then you will lose your reader. Keep it simple. On most of my proposal covers, I only use one image. In project sheets and resumes, I use one image for the project and one image for the team member. In addition, limit the color palette and the number of fonts. Do your best to keep it simple.

Relevant

Your graphics must be relevant to the subject matter. I once had an extensive argument with a project executive because he didn't understand why I had pictures of college students on the front cover of a construction services proposal. A large majority of the RFP specified how important student safety was to the overall success of the proposal. In addition, at the pre-bid meeting, more emphasis was placed on the students and student safety. Although we were a construction company, we were doing the work on a very busy college campus, and the end users were the students and staff. I felt it was important that we communicated through the cover art that we were aware of who the end users were and how important it was that we kept them safe. In other portions of the proposal, I included photographs of our construction team, but I thought it was more important to make sure the review staff understood that we knew their students and staff were our clients as well.

In the proposal below, RSA (a lobbying firm) was pursuing a lobbying contract with the Pinellas Suncoast Transit Authority (PSTA). RSA's interest in serving a public organization that serves its public is captured by the image of two women riding on a bus.

9.7 Proposal Cover.

In the example below, a software development team submitted a RFP response for website design and hosting services. The end users were teachers, parents, and kids. With the end users in mind, the proposal covers and tabs incorporated the various users of the technology solution.

9.8 Proposal covers and tabs for a company selling wireless services to a K-12 public school district.

Useful

When you incorporate tables or graphics in your proposals, make sure they are useful. Organizational charts are a good example of a useful graphic, as well as project schedules and process maps.

In the example below, images of the staff are included in the organizational chart as well as images representing the core functions the team would provide services for.

Remember, selection committees have to read thousands of pages and try to remember details about each team. Make it easy for the selection committee to remember you by creating graphics that are useful and help them easily absorb the information in your proposal.

9.9 Organizational chart with contract phases as well as color codes for the prime contractor and sub-consultant.

Focused

Graphics included in your proposal should be more than just "pretty." Your graphics should be focused and represent information the RFP requests. In the example below, the RFP asked for "a graphic representation of your current commitment over the next year for key members of the project team, and we designed the graphic below to illustrate the team's capacity over the next year.

29. Provide a graphic representation of your current commitment over the next one year period for key members of the project team.

The following graphic illustrates Sourcetoad's commitment over the next one year period for key members of the project team.

■ 100% commitment to the Hillsborough County Surface Water Quality Database Website project.

□ 25% - 50% commitment to the Hillsborough County Surface Water Quality Database Website project.

Team Member	Project Role	August 2014	September 2014	October 2014	November 2014	December 2014	January 2015	February 2015	March 2015	April 2015	May 2015	June 2015	July 2015
Greg Ross-Munro	Sr. Project Manager												
Nick DeMelas	Project Manager												
David Eddy	Sr. Developer												
Adam Husarek	Developer												
Leon McIntosh	Developer												

9.10 Employee workload matrix.

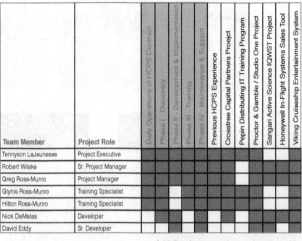

9.11 Employee past experience matrix.

Captions

Make sure you make the most of your relevant images by adding great captions that describe what is happening in the image. In APMP's "Proposal Writing for Dummies", the authors encourage the use of "action captions." Action captions are, "One complete sentence that explains the relevance of the graphic to the evaluator, linking benefits to features. The simpler you can make an action caption, the better."

In the image and caption below, I used the action caption to describe proposed team members wrapping up a project. The image shows the team behind the software, which shows the selection committee they are buying more than just a product, they're buying a team of local talent.

Above - Our Tampa-based team going above and beyond to quickly perform QC on the XYZ App for a few new custom features requested by the client.

9.12 Image and caption example.

Envisioning Success

Graphics are a great way to give your readers less text to absorb and help your proposal stand out from your competition. Make sure you use relevant graphics, tables, and images to reiterate key points in your proposal. Keep your graphics focused on answering the questions asked in the RFP, and use captions to describe what your images are depicting. If you can create a great balance between text and graphics in your proposal, your team will be one step closer to the shortlist presentation.

Quality Control and Review

It's happened to all of us: you've spent the last week working on a proposal only to find a grammatical error on the first page of your proposal the day after you've submitted it to a client. Proper spelling, grammar, and punctuation on proposals is critical. If you submit a proposal that is filled with errors and isn't written clearly, then it immediately causes problems for the reader. The selection committee member reviewing your proposal may instantly start to mistrust the information in your submittal, and he or she may think, "If this vendor can't even take the time to edit their own proposal, I wonder how they'll perform on this contract?" Make the selection members trust your company by submitting a proposal with fewer errors.

In this section, we'll discuss quality control for your proposals and methods you can use to find mistakes in your proposal before your client does.

The Do-it-Yourself Guide

If you are a marketing and business development team of one, work in a small firm, or have a deadline close to a holiday, you may have to do the quality control for the proposal yourself. Here are a few tips to help you out:

1. **Give yourself some distance.** I've found that a little bit of distance or time away from the proposal can give you the best chance of finding your own mistakes. If possible, get the proposal draft done before a weekend or build in a few days where you don't have to look at the proposal content. When you come back from a few days off, you'll be surprised what errors instantly spring off the page.
2. **Review the proposal backwards.** Don't review the proposal front to back, instead, look at it in reverse. You'll be surprised how many issues you can find when you read content in inverse order.
3. **Break it apart.** If you know ahead of time that you will be doing a lot of the review yourself for a proposal, try to get a project approach or the more technical components of your proposal done way in advance and have the appropriate person at your firm review them. The proposal and review process doesn't necessarily have to be a linear process.
4. **Change the format.** I like to cut and paste sections into a different Word document and then enlarge the font to a point size 24 or higher. I do this for two reasons: (1) When the content is in a different format, I can sometimes spot mistakes I didn't see before; and (2) the larger font slows me down. It's hard to find mistakes when you're skimming through a proposal. To really slow down and find your own mistakes, changing the format can help you spot more issues.

5. **Keep asking yourself, "so what?"** As you review the proposal, ask, "so what?" over and over again. When you continually ask yourself this question, you are making sure that you keep the proposal focused on the client and the project. If your proposal is filled with a lot of boilerplate, you may find yourself re-writing your content so it specifically addresses the benefit to the client. For example, "Our firm has been in the Raleigh area for more than 50 years." So what? The re-write might look something like this, "Our firm has been in the Raleigh area for more than 50 years, which has helped us form long-term relationships with only the best-performing subcontractors in the market." With the re-write, you can see why having 50 years of experience in the area can really benefit the client.

6. **Don't get too attached to your content.** It's easy to get attached to your proposal content when you've spent so much time digging up and researching past experience, or crafting narrative that sounds fantastic. The bottom line is, if it doesn't directly help the client see why your firm is the best fit for a project or build on your win themes, then it doesn't belong in the proposal. Sometimes deleting content that you really worked hard on is one of the toughest choices you'll have to make during the quality control process.

Performing Quality Control with a Team

If you have a proposal team involved in writing and reviewing the proposal, then you need to work in adequate review time into your proposal schedule. Similar to how you learned how to write for all audiences in the previous section, you want to create a review process that can spot errors for both technical and non-technical readers.

1. **Giver your proposal team time to review the proposal and submit their changes.** One person should be responsible for incorporating all of the edits. If I'm working with a team that's all in-house, then I print out one draft and circulate it to the entire team, ending with the most senior person. If I'm working with a remote team, I use a PDF version and send it out but I only let one person review at a time before sending it to the next person. By letting one person review at a time, I make sure that I don't get conflicting changes. Based on the timeline, you may not have enough time to send it to everyone who contributed content. If that's the case, submit it to only a select few and still try to get comments from one person before sending it to the next person.

2. **Keep access to the proposal limited.** Depending on how big your team is or their technical aptitude, I highly recommend restricting access to one person. I have seen proposal content disappear. I have seen people accidentally delete files, and it isn't pretty. Any quality control process really works best when one person has access to the

entire proposal document. If team members want to work on editing a document together, then post that content to a shared document (like a Google Doc) and let the team edit it there and then paste it into the final proposal document. Do not let your entire team have access to the proposal document.

3. **Find additional reviewers that weren't involved in writing the proposal.** It's important that you find both technical and non-technical staff to review the proposal. You also should have a principal or a very senior member of the management team to review the proposal and give their feedback. Give each reviewer a copy of the RFP, the RFP response, and a comment sheet. I advise the reviewers to make any comments on the draft and to fill out the comment sheet. I keep the comment sheet simple:

   - Did we answer all of the questions or was there anything we missed?
   - List three reasons why our team should win the project. (Determines if the reviewer picked up on our three win themes.)
   - What would you change if you were writing any part of the proposal responses?

4. **Discourage last-minute moments of brilliance.** Sometimes, during the final review of a high-stakes proposal, a principal or senior manager will have a flash of insight or a "last-minute moment of brilliance" that strikes him or her a few hours or a day before the proposal is due. I have rewritten and reworked parts of a proposal at the 11th hour based on these moments. Usually these insights are not helpful. If a last-minute change is requested that drastically affects the overall proposal, question the person wanting to make the change. Gently remind the principal or senior manager that your company performed adequate pre-sell for the project and the approach, team, and qualifications as outlined in the proposal are a result of this pre-sell effort. Abandoning the plan at this late hour may not be the best idea and may instead be the result of some nervous energy.

Keep Striving

The most important factor of any quality control or review process is consistency. The proposal team and proposal reviewers should be trained on what to look for in the proposal response (consider asking them to read the "Writing for All Audiences" section). The most important part of the review process is that you and your team get comfortable in receiving feedback and have a process for incorporating it back into the draft. No proposal is perfect, but if you follow some of the suggestions in this section, it will save you from the pain of having your client find them for you.

SUMMARY

In this chapter, you learned how to make your proposals stand out from your competition. When you work on your next proposal, remember to do the following:

- Be aware that your audience will include technical and non-technical readers. Make sure your proposal writing speaks to both audiences.
- Help your reader understand your proposal better by being concise, using headings, graphics, tables, and staying within the page limit (the selection committee has a lot of reading to do).
- During proposal production: outsource covers and tabs, don't print the day the proposal is due, and print early!
- When collaborating with a team: create a project team contact sheet to help with team coordination, take time to brainstorm, control your documents, and know the hierarchy for document changes.
- Use grids to make your page layouts consistent and aesthetically pleasing.
- Keep your proposal graphics relevant, useful, and focused in order to make the most impact on the selection committee.
- Make sure you leave enough time in your proposal production schedule for quality control and review.

Now that you know how to create high-impact proposals, it's important to understand what comes next in the process after you submit the proposal.

10

10

POST-PROPOSAL SUBMISSION

 According to most studies, people's number one fear is public speaking. Number two is death. Death is number two. Does that sound right? This means to the average person, if you go to a funeral, you're better off in the casket than delivering the eulogy."

Jerry Seinfeld

Shortlist Presentations

There are many consultants in the business world offering high-level and expensive presentation classes to executives. There is a good reason for this: presentations can make or break a deal. If your team doesn't connect with the selection committee on a personal level, then your firm might lose a deal. Depending on the total amount of the contract, private companies or agencies may opt for a presentation to make a final decision on which firm should be awarded a project contract. In this section, I'm going to give you a few tips on presentation preparation and delivery.

What You Need to Know Before You Start Planning Your Presentation
Before you start planning your presentation, it's a good idea to know a little about the room you'll be presenting in. You may want to ask a few questions like:

- What kind of room will we be presenting in?
- How many people are we presenting to?
- Will there be a projector in the room?
- Will there be a screen in the room?
- Will there be a laptop available? Is it PC or Mac?
- Can we see the room ahead of time?

Planning the Presentation

After responding to an RFP, you're probably thinking: "What else can we possibly tell them?" The shortlist presentation isn't really an opportunity to present new information, as much as it is an opportunity to hit on the three key win themes your firm emphasized in the RFP response. Why should the client pick your team and not your competitor? When you're planning your presentation, you should focus on at least three main points. Keep it simple. In some cases, the selection committee may have 15 other firms they're listening to as well. You can imagine how hard it would be for a selection committee to listen to similar presentations 15 times in a row.

In order to clarify your key points, presentation style, and other details, it's a good idea to have a kick-off meeting for the presentation preparation as well. Just as you created a proposal matrix (Chapter 8), do the same thing for the presentation preparation process.

Presentation Format

Depending on the agency and selection committee, they may have a list of criteria they would like you to address during your presentation. Make sure you address all of these items as well as the three points of differentiation. A basic presentation starts with an overview of what you're going to present, the meat of the presentation (team, experience, approach, budget, schedule), and a conclusion.

How Many People Should Do the Presentation?
For most presentations, no more than three people from your team should present. Carol Sheafnocker, a former boss of mine and an industry veteran of more than 30 years, always emphasized that each person in the presentation must have a role. Depending on the complexity of the project and the dollar value, you may need to bring in the entire 20-person team and sub-consultants. Generally, two to three people doing a 20-30 minute presentation is adequate. Each person must have something of value to contribute.

Rehearse, Rehearse, Rehearse!
I have never worked with a project team that wanted to rehearse. Chances are, neither will you. Again, like Louise Ellrod says, you will need to be "professionally persistent" to get your team to rehearse. Carol Scheafnocker advises, "Take charge, demand rehearsals. There is nothing worse than a team presenting to a client without practicing. I never let that happen. A bad presentation is very hard to overcome for the marketing person."

If you can get your team to do three practice runs, you're doing great. I am usually happy once I get a terrible rehearsal. I like to think that if we can get the terrible rehearsal out of the way, it won't happen when we do the actual presentation. Another important reason your team needs to rehearse is because presenting may not be a normal activity for your team, so it will need practice. You wouldn't see a professional football team show up without having the plays practiced and memorized, so why would your presentation team show up any differently?

Deliverables and Presentation Style
Although PowerPoint is a great presentation tool, you don't always need to use it for a great presentation. What if, when you spoke to the procurement contact, he or she mentioned the presentation room has a bad internet connection or that the projector doesn't always work that well? You may consider presentation books or boards. No matter the format, don't let technology prevent your team from giving a great presentation. When you're rehearsing, try doing a run-through one time without the PowerPoint working. This is always a great test for how well your team knows the presentation!

Placemats

One of my favorite presentation leave-behinds is an 11 x 17 folded to 8.5 x 11 that gives a brief overview of your presentation. Below are a couple of examples. This leave-behind features a cover, agenda, organizational chart, summary of project experience and past clients, as well as a condensed copy of the PowerPoint presentation.

10.0 Page 1 of leave-behind.

10.1 Page 2 of leave-behind.

Connection is Key

The most important part of your presentation is your team connecting with the selection committee. Part of the reason rehearsals are so important is so that your team stops worrying about what they're going to say (because they know it) and instead focuses on reading and responding to the prospective client.

What Makes for a Great Presentation

The previous section talked more about the logistics and approach for creating a presentation. This section now focuses on what constitutes a great presentation. Great presentations follow three core principles:

- Great presentations are focused on a win theme;
- Great presentations are customized for the prospective client's project; and
- Great presentations demonstrate a passion for the project.

Win Theme Focused

In earlier chapters, we talked about establishing your differentiators and then incorporating them into your win theme. After you use these components in your cover letter, executive summary, and proposal content, you want to make sure you incorporate them again into your presentation.

Great Presentations Are Customized for the Project and Prospective Client

Have you ever sat in a presentation that was a series of the speaker reading out from 30 text-heavy PowerPoint slides? It's painful, isn't it? Clearly, the presenter didn't really give a lot of thought to the poor soul who would have to listen to him reading out his slides. You shouldn't do this to your client if you have a 45-minute presentation. After you've done a little discovery on the room set up and received topics of conversation from your client, make sure you create a customized presentation that sells all of your key points in an engaging way. Do not take a previous presentation and start editing it for your current pursuit. I encourage you to try an approach as outlined by Garr Reynolds in his book "Presentation Zen: Simple Ideas on Presentation Design and Delivery". Reynolds outlines a process for creating great presentations and PowerPoint slides. A lot of his process focuses on stepping away from your computer and first drafting or sketching your presentation on paper, storyboarding it (again on paper), and then moving your presentation to a digital form.

Feel Free to Ditch PowerPoint

Have you ever gone on a date or a business meeting and the person you're with keeps checking their cell phone? How do you feel? I know I get a little frustrated if that kind of behavior goes on for quite a while. Based on that behavior, think about how you and your team may let technology get in the way of connecting with your audience.

Depending on the room set up for your presentation, you may or may not want to use a PowerPoint presentation. I know when you see "presentation," you think "PowerPoint" but I'd like to see you get out of that mind set. Remember, your key focus is to connect with your prospective client. I've seen great presentations created using only large foam-core boards or simple paper handouts.

Great Presentations Have a Customized Approach

Creating a customized presentation means you examine everything involved with the presentation and ask your team how this helps the prospective client understand and connect with your message. Another component of a customized presentation is a customized project approach. In "How to Win a Pitch," author Joey Asher addresses a common concern he faces with his clients. Most of his clients are worried about giving away their approach for free, "When I tell my clients that they need to detail their specific solution to the business problems in their presentation, many object and say, 'That's giving away free advice.' My response is, 'You give away the plan, but you charge them for the implementation.'" Don't let your fear of giving away a powerful, customized project approach lose your competitive advantage for winning your next project.

Great Presentations Demonstrate a Passion for the Project

It doesn't matter if you and your team have practiced for weeks. It does, however, matter if your team can convey its passion for the project at hand. I've been involved with presentations for universities that allow all competitors to watch each other's presentations. For one particular large university project, I saw each of my competitor's presentations.

Although my team was well prepared, the winning firm had a superintendent that basically screamed at the selection committee with his enthusiasm for the project - and the selection committee felt it. Shortly after the presentations, each of the competing firms was invited to sit in on the deliberation for the project award. Sure enough, qualifications aside, the selection committee was overwhelmingly impressed by the passion conveyed by the superintendent. After all, he was the one who was going to build the project and interact with the staff through the duration of the project. This superintendent's presentation performance weighed heavily on the selection committee's minds.

Now I'm not saying that your team has to scream at the selection committee to get your firm's next job, but conveying your passion and enthusiasm for the project is important. Make sure each person presenting has a very personal reason why this project will make a difference in his or her life. For example, "I'm a graduate of this university and working on the campus again would be very fulfilling." If each member on your team knows their own "why" for the project, it will really help your team in selling themselves for the project.

Passion + Focus = Success

Creating a great presentation that will help your team win its next job can be incredibly exciting. Remember to be focused on your team's win themes, customize your presentation, and demonstrate a clear passion for the project. If your team uses these three principles, it will help your firm quickly organize information and present much better than the competition.

Debriefing

Win or lose, you need to debrief. Your firm may have spent countless hours meeting with the prospective client or agency, drafting an RFP response, and preparing a great presentation, only to find out that you lost. Or better, your firm worked through the same process and you found out that you won. Either way, debriefing helps you understand how your prospect makes a decision and what they thought of the service offering your firm provided. Feedback or a debrief about your sales process is basically free business consulting. Use any feedback you get to improve your sales process, key messaging, and sales skills.

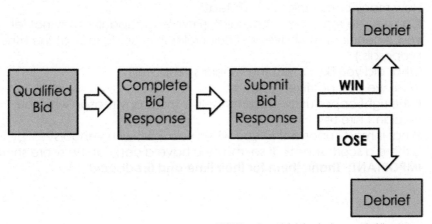

10.2 Win or lose, debriefing is always part of the process.

How to Approach the Debrief

First, you'll need to contact the client or the agency to schedule a time for a debrief. Face-to-face is preferable over a phone meeting. If your firm lost the pursuit, the email might sound something like: "Thank you again for the opportunity to present on XYZ project. Although it may not be the result we would have liked, we'd still like to work towards earning a future project. A great way for us to improve is to conduct a debrief with your firm/agency so we can improve our marketing efforts and service offering. With that said, would you mind giving us a short 30-minute meeting in person so we can ask you a few questions about our RFP response as well as our presentation?" After that, I give three dates two to three weeks in the future. The purpose of the email is to let the prospective client know we are not angry about the outcome and that they are not going to get any harsh questions from us.

If your firm won the pursuit, the best time to do a debrief is at your first meeting with the client. It doesn't have to be a formal process, it can be a simple open-ended question like, "There was a lot of competition for this project. What ultimately made you decide to go with us? We're always looking to improve. Is there something we could do better next time?"

No matter what the client says to you, make sure you listen. Don't interrupt, make excuses, or complain about the outcome.

Debrief Questions to the Prospective Client

Below are a few debrief questions you can ask the client. Some of them may make more sense at a project debrief for a project you didn't win.

- Did we follow all of the requirements? Could we have been more compliant in any section?
- How many companies competed?
- Can we see the other proposals? (Private companies may not let you. Agencies may have particular rules in order to look at the other proposals.)
- What did you like about the winner's proposal?
- Were we competitively priced?
- If the right opportunity presents itself, is there any reason why you wouldn't hire us?
- What is most important to you when you work with vendors?
- Is there a score sheet? If so, may we have a copy of the score sheet?
- **IMPORTANT: Thank them for their time and feedback!**

Internal Debrief

Depending on the size of your firm, you may want to have an internal debrief with your project team after you have a debrief with the client. Again, this isn't the time to assign blame to a team member who dropped the ball. An internal debrief should be a conversation and an opportunity to look at ways to improve your marketing process so that your firm can compete better next time. Here are a few questions that you might want to start with:

- Should we have gone after this RFP?
- Did we follow all of the requirements?
- How can we improve the quality of our next response?
- Is there boilerplate we can prepare for future proposals?
- How can we reduce the amount of time we spend on proposals?
- What can we differentiate ourselves better from the competition?

Debriefing is a fantastic tool to help your team continually improve and learn how to better sell your company's services. The only way to fail at debriefing is to not do it. So after your next pursuit, give it a try!

Post-Proposal and Presentation Submittal

After you've conducted client and internal debriefs, you probably have a good idea of how you can make some immediate improvements to your resumes, project sheets, and RFP response narrative, as well as a few ways to improve your PowerPoint presentation for the next time. Make sure you make these improvements while they're still fresh in your mind because chances are your next proposal is right around the corner. If your company has a Customer Relationship Management (CRM) system or a Proposal Management System, update information in the respective system so that you're already ahead of the game for your next proposal.

Recycle and Reuse Content

The good news is that after you've gone through this proposal process, you now have some great materials that you can repurpose and reuse. Perhaps in the most recent proposal, you created content for three new projects your firm is working on. Not all of the information you obtained for your proposal should be posted online. Make sure you take out specific client contact and pricing information you don't want to made public. After you've scrubbed your content, you're now ready to repurpose this content for blog posts on your website. Here's how:

- **Break up the content.** First, create three separate "Project Highlight" blog posts for each respective project. All of the information you gathered for these projects is rich with search engine key words and this information will be fantastic for your company website. Once you have done a little editing and added a few quotes about the project from your project team, post this information on your blog.

- **Parse it out.** Next, plan to release one new project highlight each week for three weeks. For SEO purposes, it's best if you consistently release new content on a regular basis. Search engines regularly check the blog posts on your website and know that when people are looking for information, they want the most current information available. Make sure that you are consistently posting interesting content to your website's blog page.

- **Distribute on social media.** When you post each blog, you can also post status updates on Facebook, LinkedIn, and Twitter, linking back to the blog post you just released. Remember, these posts create inbound links to your website, which raises your search engine optimization. In the case of Twitter, you can create multiple posts for the same content. Let's say that you posted a project highlight about a 30,000-square foot retail facility your company just finished construction on. You might post three tweets a day linking to your project for a few days, and you could change the tweets like this:
  - Finished right on time for Christmas. Check out our newest #retail center! #Builder [link to project blog];@Client Great retail project great team to work with! #Retail #builder [link to project blog]; or
  - Where are you doing your Christmas shopping? Try the ABC shopping center we just finished! [Link to project blog].

- **Get Your team to share on social media.** When you add new content to your website, make sure you get the other employees to share the content as well. Chances are, a lot of them would like their family and friends to know more about the cool projects they work on. Simply send out a link to the content to your employees via email and tell them to share the content. Believe it or not, some people may still not check some of their social media accounts on a regular basis or be following your company's social media. Emailing your staff and getting them involved is a great way to grow your social media presence from the inside out.

10

SUMMARY

In this chapter, you learned what happens after you submit your proposal and how to:

- Make sure you and your team are prepared for the shortlist presentation;
- Create great presentations that are tailored to your prospective client's project;
- Conduct a debrief with a client or agency; and
- Reuse content you generated through the proposal development process.

In the next chapter, we'll talk about technology and tools to make your job a little easier.

11
TECHNOLOGY AND TOOLS

 The technology keeps moving forward, which
makes it easier for the artists to tell their stories
and paint the pictures they want."
George Lucas

Where to Start with Digital Media

In addition to Business Development and Marketing for a small to medium-sized firm, you may also be required to tackle digital media strategies. You'll notice that I've gone into this subject last. A lot of marketing consultants will tell you to start with your digital marketing strategy. Marketing consultants will also tell you that you must stay relevant by having a continually changing blog on your website, social media posts 24 hours a day, and a stream of great content for your target clients.

Unfortunately, that's probably not the best way to immediately make a positive first impression with your new boss and your new professional services company. When you sell a professional service, it's critical to focus on the immediate needs of your repeat clients. After you have a solid business development and proposal management process in place, then it's time to turn your attention to digital media.

Websites

Your website is your digital storefront. Chances are, your firm already has a website. Depending on how the website was created, you may be able to change things without extensive coding skills. Let's assume you're dealing with a website that is only updated by a webmaster and you don't have any ability to change it - that's okay. Eventually, you want to work towards a website that allows you to make changes easily as big events happen for your firm. If your company has the budget for a marketing or website development company to manage the changes for you, that's great! In more recent years, I've had to help manage a lot of the website content myself.

Refreshing Your Website

If you are in the same shoes I was and need to manage the website content yourself, the tool that you want to learn more about is a Content Management System (CMS). A CMS is the system that manages website content behind the scenes. CMS tools help you manage your content so you don't have to learn HTML, CSS, or JavaScript to make changes to website content. You may need to do a little research to find a CMS you like working with. There are a variety of CMS tools in the marketplace, but my favorite is WordPress. I've updated four websites: one had a Drupal CMS and the other three were websites built with a Wordpress CMS. If you are not a technical person or do not want to learn how to code (like me), you will probably like WordPress.

If you know what kind of CMS you want to use, you can probably go to most marketing and website design firms and ask them for help to convert your old site to a new WordPress site. Remember: you get what you pay for. Based on the type of website refresh you want, you can get estimates anywhere from $1,000 to $50,000. Make sure you do a little research and review each company's work as part of your due diligence process. The right website consultant can really help you shape your company's messaging in a way that will help improve your Search Engine Optimization (SEO) rankings.

Be Careful with Your Firm's Website Graphics

Make sure that you are careful with any photography and graphics you use on your website. For example, if your firm is a general contracting firm, don't use Google street images of completed projects as project photography unless you directly link to it. An acceptable Google link would be linking to a map showing your office location. If at all possible, take images yourself or hire a photographer to get some great project or team photos. Stock photography is also another good option. There are a couple of free websites for stock photography, but I prefer to use some of the more reputable sites for graphics and photos. One of my favorite stock photography websites is Thinkstock (www.thinkstock.com). You can get photography and fantastic illustrations.

What is SEO and Why Should I Care?

In short, Search Engine Optimization (SEO) is how clients find companies like yours to provide the services they need. Every search engine out there (Google, Explorer, Bing), is essentially an advertising company. Each search engine scours and "reads" every website each night (also known as indexing). When a person goes to Google and types in "Best Accounting Firms in Atlanta, Georgia," Google has evaluated through its complicated formula or algorithm company websites that have the information the person is looking for. Your goal is to get as close as you can to the top of the list by having key features on your website that help the Google search engine rank you the highest. Features that help with a higher SEO ranking include things like inbound links, content that changes often (i.e., blog), and so on. To make sure your company gets ranked higher in the search results, you can always pay for an ad, but that can get expensive. By creating great content on your website and sharing links via social media, you can rank higher without having to pay high advertising fees.

Maintaining Your Website

Now that you understand a little about SEO, you can use your blog to boost your website's SEO. You'll want to write blog articles for the following: when your company wins a project; your firm hires a new employee; or you or a member from your firm attends a great industry event and wants to share some interesting information. You want to aim for one blog post a month and one a week when you're really rolling. A blog is not the place to put news that is more personal in nature (for example: one of the project managers at your firm is a new parent). You want to save personal employee news for your company's Facebook page.

Google Analytics

A great way to determine how your website is performing and how people are finding your site is to use Google Analytics. There is tons of information you can access online to help you understand how to use Google Analytics including a course offered by Google: https://analyticsacademy.withgoogle.com/.

How Does Social Media and Email Blasts Tie into a Digital Marketing Strategy?

Remember how inbound links help raise a website's SEO? That's why email blasts and social media is important. LinkedIn, Facebook, YouTube, Instagram, Pinterest, and Twitter can be used to create inbound links to content on your website, which proves to be a useful tool for raising your site's SEO. In the rest of this section, I'll give you a little insight on how to use each social media channel.

LinkedIn

A LinkedIn company page is a great tool to have, but each of your firm's employees sharing content that you post on your website is better. Make sure each of the key staff for your firm has a LinkedIn profile and shares new content from your website when you post it.

Facebook

The best way to use a Facebook company page is as an internal company website that helps represent your company's culture. A company Facebook page is a great way to share news about company employees and their families (if the employees are okay with it). A Facebook company page is a great place to announce employee: marriages, births, awards, etc. You can also post industry relevant news, project wins, and new hires. You'd be surprised how many proud parents and spouses will follow your employees' company Facebook page. Take advantage of that!

YouTube and Vimeo

Company training videos, messages from the company president, and other cool things that happen at your company are great for video sharing sites like YouTube and Vimeo.

Twitter

Believe it or not, Twitter is probably one of the best tools available for competitive research. I love to check out my competitors and see who they're following and what they're tweeting about. Checking out your competition is also a good way to determine who you should be following and what kinds of things you may want to post about.

When it comes to what you should be posting on Twitter, I like to maintain a ratio of 80/20 when it comes to sharing industry-relevant content to my own firm's content. It's better to share and comment on relevant topics than constantly pushing your own content. It's the equivalent to going to a dinner party and talking about yourself the entire time. No one wants to sit next to the self-centered bore. If you talk about topics that people like to hear about 80% of the time and interject smaller nuggets about yourself, it's a better way to make friends and, in Twitter's case, get followers. When it comes to connecting on Twitter, make sure you keep your ratios in check in terms of following and followers. Because social media changes every day, you may want to do a little research online to see what the proper following/follower ratio guidelines are.

Managing Social Media Accounts

Managing multiple social media accounts for your firm and sometimes your key staff can be challenging. One of the best tools I've found for managing multiple social media accounts is Buffer (www.buffer.com). Hootsuite (hootsuite.com) is another great option and works well for marketing firms that manage social media for multiple clients. You can get great results by using Buffer if you're a smaller firm and don't have a large marketing budget. Hootsuite tends to itemize charges for its various reports while Buffer offers you a lot of the reports you need as part of the monthly subscription. The bottom line is: if you're posting to multiple social media accounts, you're going to need a tool to help you do that.

When it comes to monitoring all of your platforms, visit each respective account at least once a week (and in some cases, once a day) to make sure all of the content displaying is relevant to your firm. Social media accounts can occasionally get hacked so checking them periodically is a good way to make sure your company's reputation stays on track. It's also good to check them on a regular basis so you can share content from your friends and followers.

Social Media Tone and Etiquette

A social media account should be a positive reflection of your company's culture. At the same time, a lot of social media platforms were designed with individuals in mind. The question then becomes, "How do I maintain a unique style without sounding too dull or too 'corporate' so I can get engagement?" With a little bit of practice, trial and error, you can figure out how to find your company's social media voice. The good news is that you can usually find out how well you're doing with this based on the number of likes, follows, or shares you get. It takes time to grow an audience for your firm. Honesty, persistence and message refinement will get you to higher social media engagement. Lots of original pictures help, too!

The Bad of Social Media

Although social media utilization can be a positive tactic to help raise your firm's SEO, it can also work against your company if you're not vigilant. At one of my previous companies, one employee's actions created a little bit of a nightmare when he commented on another woman's page about a very personal issue. Because I didn't have the correct settings on Facebook, this woman posted a lot of comments that were inappropriate, to say the least. Fortunately, we quickly resolved the issue. Be cognizant of your social media settings and who's posting. If it's not you, make sure that someone is monitoring your presence on a regular basis.

Email Marketing

If your company has a list of past clients and contacts that exceeds 200 people, don't use your regular email account to send email blasts. Once your firm hits 200 people, it's time to start using an email service like Constant Contact (www.constantcontact.com) or MailChimp (www. mailchimp.com) to send your email blasts. Both services have great reporting metrics so you can see who's opening and reading your emails as well as what links they're clicking on. Make sure you that you tie your email blasts to your website so you get more SEO bang for your buck!

SPAM and Unsubscribing

If you're not familiar with the CAN-SPAM Act, you should check out Constant Contact's website since it has some great information about spam and how to comply with the legislation. Basically, if you have permission to email people and you're not trying to be misleading, you're probably safe. But to make sure you're compliant with your email communications and unsubscribe functions, you may want to give the information a quick read through at: http://support2.constantcontact.com/articles/FAQ/1728.

Proposal Software

After you've completed a few RFP responses, you'll realize you've been answering the same RFP questions repeatedly. You know you've written a paragraph in a previous proposal and it's somewhere in your computer. Where is it? It's becoming clear that you need to systematize some part of your proposal process, otherwise you'll go insane. Congratulations! You've experienced enough pain and you're now ready to choose a proposal software platform to help you fix your proposal insanity (trust me, I'm laughing with you). Before you choose your proposal software, I have a few tips for you.

1. **Don't implement a system in the middle of your busiest time of the year for proposals.** You may think you'll increase productivity if you can automate the process as quickly as possible, but you won't. When you decide to change the way you respond to RFQs or RFPs, there is a very steep learning curve. The first few times you use the new software, it can take you double the amount of time it usually does to assemble a proposal.
2. **Analyze the types of clients you serve.** Consider the client types of the RFQs and RFPs you typically respond to. There are some great tools out there for responding to private companies as well as some excellent tools to use when responding to government, municipalities, or other public clients. Picking the right type of software designed to work according to your client's specifications can make a huge difference in your overall productivity.
3. **Think about the deliverables your clients typically want.** Do you do more print proposals or electronic submittals? Some software solutions are better for purely digital deliverables while others work much better for paper submittals.
4. **Consider software systems your industry currently uses.** When I was in the healthcare IT space, PMAPS was a popular system, while in the architectural, engineering, and construction (A/E/C) industries, Deltek Vision is the standard for larger firms, but Cosential is the perfect choice for smaller or medium-sized firms based on the price point. If you use the right proposal platform for your industry, it will be easier to find staff who know how to use it and this will lessen the learning curve. Recently, I've come across RFP365, which has some great functionality for both procurement teams and bidders.

5. **Think about how many people in your firm will be creating proposals or involved in the process.** If you're a small firm but are planning to grow in the next year, the type of system you implement may be very different from the firm with three offices and 15 people working on proposals at the same time.
6. **Do you have other systems you may want to integrate with your proposal system?** In the A/E/C Industry, it's beneficial for the marketing coordinator and/or marketing department to have access to financial data. Thus, a system that can integrate with your existing financial system is incredibly useful to eliminate manual data entry.
7. **Cost.** You'll notice I bring this up last. If you really have no budget to implement a proposal system, then focus on staying more organized with your content so that when you do have a budget large enough to get the system, you pick one that will stick with you as you grow. Remember, with many software platforms, some configuration is usually required and that can cost you a few thousand dollars before the monthly or yearly subscription rate.

Other Proposal Software Considerations

Proposal software is only as good as the existing proposal systems in place. If you're looking to get a proposal system in the hopes that it will get you organized, you're going to be facing a losing battle. In the pre-proposal preparation section, I discussed a procedure to make sure you were getting the most up-to-date information on your projects. If you haven't been maintaining your process at this level, I highly recommend that you first master that aspect before moving on to implementing a proposal system.

Customer Relationship Management (CRM) Software

Customer Relationship Management (CRM) systems are a great addition to any functioning marketing department and are my favorite tool to implement. However, a CRM is only as good as the information that's fed into it. There are a lot of CRM systems on the market now. Below, I'll talk about some of my favorite aspects of different types of tools you can use to organize your contact information and the pros and cons associated with each.

Outlook

I have joined many firms that use Outlook as their primary source to store client contact information. The bad part about not having a centralized contact management system is it's not sharable among employees in real time. If your firm only uses Outlook, there will be times when you'll reach out to a client about something only to have that client tell you that another employee just reached out to them about a similar issue a few days ago. Making sure that you have a contact system that can serve as a shared knowledge center for all of your client information is critical to giving clients the impression that everyone in your firm is on the same page. Another issue with using a later edition of Outlook is if your system gets hacked, you lose a lot of time trying to get that information back.

Mass Email Solutions

Some firms use systems like Constant Contact (www.constantcontact.com), Mail Chimp (https://mailchimp.com/), or Emma (http://myemma.com/) to manage their client contacts. Although this format is more sharable than Outlook and is backed up in the cloud, it doesn't track other types of information that may be useful to other employees in your firm (including your marketing and business development team).

Project Specific CRMs for Smaller to Medium-Sized Firms

Several firms use tools like Pipedrive (https://www.pipedrive.com/) to manage their sales pipeline and this can be a great tool for general contractors and other types of professional services firms that track longer project pursuits. If your firm is targeting specific project work and has a very specific team that chases these types of pursuits, this may be the tool for you. Pipedrive is very easy to get up and running for your team and requires little training.

Highly Customizable and Flexible CRMs for Smaller to Medium-Sized Firms

If your firm has marketing and business development professionals as well as support staff, you may need a tool like Insightly (www.insightly.com). Insightly is one of my favorite CRMs because it is easy to customize based on your firm's workflow. I've used other enterprise level systems that don't have the functionality and customization options Insightly does. However, if you work at a larger firm, and your system has to integrate with larger accounting systems, then this might not be the best solution for you. Insightly gives all users access to information in real time, and is backed up in the cloud. You can track different types of projects and opportunities. I love the shared calendar and how you can use the calendar to track tasks and project milestones. The tagging functions and export capabilities to mass emailing solutions like Mail Chimp make it a great way to manage multiple departments with one highly customizable solution.

Enterprise CRM Solutions

When your firm has hundreds of people interacting with prospective clients on a regular basis, you may then have to start looking to use an enterprise CRM system. In the A/E/ C industry, I've used Deltek (https://www.deltek.com) and Cosential (https:// www.cosential.com/), although there are countless others out there. Implementing a CRM is a huge undertaking at any company. When your company is ready for this type of implementation, set up a task force to handle a CRM implementation on the enterprise level. If your company is a couple of hundred people strong, but your marketing team is only 10 or so and you have a 10-15 project managers that help with pursuits, utilize a system like Pipedrive and Insightly first, before trying to implement a system like Deltek or Cosential to make sure you get the best return on investment.

SUMMARY

In this chapter we discussed some of the fantastic digital marketing tools available. If you've taken the time to build a database of proposal materials and other marketing collateral, you have a great base to start from.

- **Website and Social Media.** Before you create or overhaul your website, make sure you have a plan for managing the content and social media channels. Digital marketing is important but not as important as making sure you're not abandoning your business development and proposal responsibilities.

- **Proposal Software.** When it comes to proposal software, a software solution is only as good as the existing systems in place. If you're looking to get a system in the hope that it will get you organized, you're going to be facing a losing battle. In the pre-proposal preparation section, I discussed a procedure to make sure you were getting the most up-to-date information on your projects. If you haven't been maintaining your process at this level, I highly recommend that you first master that aspect before moving on to implementing a proposal system.

- **CRMs.** Customer Relationship Managers (CRMs) are a great tool to help you organize your contacts and project information. Before you implement a CRM, make sure you have a good understanding of all the other systems you may need to integrate with and make sure your IT staff is on board.

With your digital marketing and technology tools taken care of, let's talk more about your firm's public relations efforts and tradeshows in the next chapter.

TRADESHOWS, TOURNAMENTS, AND PUBLIC RELATIONS

If a young man tells his date how handsome, smart and successful he is - that's advertising. If the young man tells his date she's intelligent, looks lovely, and is a great conversationalist, he's saying the right things to the right person and that's marketing. If someone else tells the young woman how handsome, smart, and successful her date is - that's PR."

S.H. Simmons

Tradeshows

Engagement is key to making an impact at your next tradeshow. Many marketers talk about engagement, but what does good engagement really feel like? The answer: fun! Good engagement is a bright chalk-colored hopscotch drawn on the sidewalk that lures the neighborhood kids to stop by and play with you. Good engagement feels like a Sharpie on slick paper. Engagement inspires curiosity and that curiosity fuels interest in your product. Be different than your booth counterparts! Don't just show up with a ton of brochures and another iPad to give away. How do you prove that you're different from your competitors? Show them. You should show you're different by demonstrating through an activity that drives engagement!

At your next medical marketing trade show, demonstrate your willingness to engage by creating a vision board for your product or service with great questions for your customers.

Discover How Your Prospective Clients Think

In Lew Hoff's www.tsnn.com article, "Tricks of the Trade Show: Engagement," he mentions how placing a greater emphasis on the entire show can greatly improve trade show engagement. So how can you do this? Incorporate ways to get real-time feedback throughout the entire show. The questions don't have to be just about your product or service. Getting a gauge on the personalities of your clients may involve some more interesting questions and an opportunity to ask more "why" questions. For example: What super hero are you? What was the first car you drove? And then you can get into the other types of questions, "I envision a construction industry that...." or "What would architecture look like without regulation?"

Make Them Feel Like a Kid Again

Your trade show experience must be fun! Monster.com uses touch screens to create an interactive experience for their trade show attendees. When interviewed in Inc., the Vice President of Monster.com Phil Cavanaugh says this about his company's interactive touch screen booth, "They don't have to wait for a guided demo...They can approach our product right away." Interactivity and a sense of "play" can engage attendees immediately and give you the opportunity to approach them in a more relaxed frame of mind.

Make Sure Your Booth Staff is Trained

Does your staff understand the importance of being engaged while in your company's booth? Part of a great trade show experience for attendees involves the interaction with your employees. Usually those employees selected to assist with the booth have sales training. However, the trade show experience may offer unique challenges that your sales staff hasn't faced before. For example, are your employees prepared to handle questions from competitors? It always helps to give your booth workers a little bit of training to ensure the trade show experience benefits your attendees and employees.

No More iPads, Bags, or Stress Balls

It's all about the experience! Don't give away another iPad, bag, or stress ball. Your trade show attendees probably have collected each of these things from another booth before visiting yours. Maybe make a statement by telling booth attendees that your company will make a $1 donation of to a charity of choice for each person who visits the booth. Are you or someone you know a great artist? Hiring someone to do a caricature at your both is a great way to talk to someone while they're getting their portrait done and your guest has something to remember your firm by when he or she goes home.

Be Disruptive by Being Traditional

Instead of spending money on another cheesy giveaway, why not invest in something a little more old-fashioned? Try following up after the trade show with a hand-written note. Yes, hand-written notes are a little more time-consuming, but if you divvy up the workload with a few of your colleagues, it can make quite an impact. You can follow up with other digital methods as well, but use the giveaway money for follow-up activities that will make a difference.

Sporting Tournaments

Tournaments for sporting clays, playing golf, or fishing are great ways to get out and interact with your existing clients as well as prospective clients. Most of these tournaments support a cause or benefit a nonprofit organization. Participating in events or tournaments is a great way to blend a little business development with doing a little good in the community. When you're selling a professional service, so much of how you do can be displayed in non-formal settings. The reason I put tournaments towards the end of the book is because if you don't have a solid foundation and strategy for your marketing and business development activities, participating in tournaments is not going to help you meet your goals. Tournaments are the types of activities you see firms engage in once they have a solid strategic plan and know how they want to make an impact in the communities they serve.

If you do work for the public sector, a great way to get to interact with these clients is to look for opportunities to contribute to causes that these organizations find valuable. It helps if your company believes in the same cause as well. If you can align your marketing efforts to support a public agency it will help you solidify the perception that your firm is one the public agency can count on to work with for years to come. This isn't an absolute, but it doesn't hurt to shine some light on your firm.

Should We Participate in Organizing a Tournament?

I recommend participating in a couple of tournaments before you decide to assist in organizing one. Once you start participating in the organization of such events, it tends to take up a great deal of your time. However, if you've attended an event for several years and you've started to see a trend in the profiles of the organizers as people that you would like to meet and do business with, you may want to consider elevating your status and participating in the planning committee. Remember to proceed with caution because these events can require a significant investment of time and you want to make sure you get the return on your investment.

Getting the Most out of Your Participation

Below, I've given three types of tournaments and some strategic suggestions for participating in each. In some cases, the type of tournament may be more geographically specific than the others (i.e., fishing tournament).

Sporting Clays Tournaments

Shooting clays or skeet shoot tournaments are quite popular in the construction and land development industries. These tournaments are expensive to host and even more expensive to attend when you consider the fees to register, staff attendance (lack of production that day), and supplies needed to participate. Usually when I've attended a sporting clays tournament, someone has been kind enough to lend me a gun and ammunition. When it's all said and done, you can expect to spend at least $2,000 - $5,000 dollars for the day for a team of four.

If you've discovered and targeted a professional organization that is hosting this type of event, and determined that it has a lot of potential clients you'd like to interact with, I can offer a few strategies for getting the most bang for your buck.

- **Hint 1: Always invite clients.** Don't plan on casually bumping into your clients at the event. If you have two employees who can attend the event, make sure that you register for four and take two potential clients with you. Do not register a team of four employees to play together. That is not going to help you! If you have four employees who would like to participate, that's great. Just make sure that you find four potential clients to take with you. The tournament can last for a couple of hours. To make the most of the money spent, make sure that you bring some potential clients.

- **Hint 2: Follow the rules.** Do your best to follow the rules as outlined in the tournament. Think about it - if you're breaking the rules and trying to win the tournament by cheating, what does that say about your firm? Also, if your client is wanting to bend the rules to win - what does that say about the type of business person he or she is? Pay attention.

- **Hint 3: Take care of your clients.** It's like a first date: pay for everything! When you invite clients to an event, make sure you have their needs taken care of. In the case of a sporting clays tournament, chances are your client will receive a shirt from the hosting organization, but it wouldn't hurt for you to have a branded vest with your company's logo to give to the client as well. Also, make sure you have enough ammunition for your clients (if it's not supplied by the tournament organizers) and a shotgun to loan them if needed. Make sure you have enough water and snacks handy for the duration of the event as well. These little details give your client a glimpse of what it would be like to work with you. Making sure all of their needs are met and they have a good time during the tournament is a great way to show them how you'd take care of them once they're your client.

- **Hint 4: Do not start nagging your prospective client for work or tips about upcoming work unless THE CLIENT brings it up.** Your clients know you paid to bring them to the tournament. They know that you would like to work with them. Don't harass them about when you can expect your next project so you can get a return on the $5,000 you just put into attending this tournament. It's just not very classy. Chances are, your client will bring it up at some point, but let them bring it up.

- **Hint 5: Follow up.** A few days after the tournament, call up your client and ask them how they enjoyed the event. If the client mentioned an upcoming project, schedule a follow-up meeting to discuss it in person.

Golf Tournaments

If you don't play golf, golf tournaments can be a little agonizing. I usually only attend if it's a scramble and I can bring someone from my firm who is a scratch golfer. Golf tournaments can range between $500-$800 for a team of four. Many of the same strategies that I recommended in the sporting clays tournament apply in this category as well, but there are a few subtle differences outlined below.

- **Hint 1: Invite clients or prospects.** Playing 18 holes can take a while, so golf tournaments are a great way to really get to know your prospect or client. If your client or prospect is a serious golfer and you're not, don't worry! Take an employee who is a great golfer. If the client is very competitive, it may be best for you to send two employees who play regularly and for you not to play at all. Plan on meeting up with the team at dinner or lunch following the tournament.

- **Hint 2: Follow the rules.** Do your best to follow the rules as outlined in the tournament. Be respectful to everyone and make sure you understand the rules of golf. Etiquette is important.

- **Hint 3: Take care of your clients.** Make sure you offer them refreshments, have plenty of extra balls and tees. You may also want to have a few branded golf accessories with your company's logo handy to give to the client (towels are nice). Alcohol in moderation is okay. If your client isn't a big drinker, it doesn't mean that you can't have an alcoholic beverage. In some cases, the client may be waiting to see if you order one before they order a drink as well. Just make sure that you don't overdo the alcohol consumption on the course. Your goal is to remember the kinds of things you and your client spoke about so you can continue to build the relationship with them in the future.

- **Hint 4: Do not start nagging your prospective client for work or tips about upcoming work unless THE CLIENT brings it up.** You're going to be on the course for quite a while. At some point, future work will probably come up. Make sure the client brings it up so they don't feel like you're bullying them into it.

- **Hint 5: Follow up.** A few days after the tournament, call up your client and ask them how they enjoyed the event. If the client mentioned an upcoming project, schedule a follow-up meeting to discuss it in person.

Fishing Tournaments

Fishing tournaments can be surprisingly expensive when you include registration fees, boat rental, captain, and bait. If your firm wants to participate in a fishing tournament, plan on spending between $3,000-$5,000. Fishing tournaments are a great way to get to know clients a little better and help them to get to know your staff. Below I've mentioned a few tips for fishing tournaments:

- **Hint 1: Invite clients or prospects.** Make sure you don't have a team of four employees going together! Ideally, you should have an even match between employees and clients so you get the most bang for your buck.

- **Hint 2: Hire a captain.** Fishing really isn't very fun if you're not catching any fish. Make sure that you hire a captain, or you take one given to you by the event organizers even if it costs extra. Listening to an expert and helping them guide you that day is worth it.

- **Hint 3: Pay extra for a boat.** If a boat can be rented the day of the event, take the organizers up on it. Even if your friend has a boat that he or she can lend to you, pay the extra for a boat. It never fails, the day of the tournament the boat's motor doesn't work, your friend didn't tell you there is no fuel in the boat, etc. You name it, and it will happen on the day of the tournament and you'll have your client watching your struggle.

- **Hint 4: Take care of your clients.** Make sure you bring some refreshments and snacks to offer your clients throughout the day. Also, you may want to have an extra shirt handy with your company's logo and a towel to give to them as well.

- **Hint 5: Don't go "fishing" for work or tips about upcoming work unless THE CLIENT brings it up.** Asking your client what projects are coming up too soon in the day could lead you to being pushed off the boat (just kidding). Make sure you give your client enough time and space to enjoy the day. The subject about work will naturally come up but let the client bring it up. Nagging your client for information could cause some tension if you initiate the conversation. Your client knows why you invited them for the tournament, chances are the subject will come up eventually.

- **Hint 6: Follow up.** A few days after the tournament, call up your client and ask them how they enjoyed the event. If the client mentioned an upcoming project, schedule a follow-up meeting to discuss it in person.

Fun Ways to Follow up After a Tournament

Probably one of my favorite ways to follow up after a tournament is to send a picture of the group my client spent the day with. You don't have to find a fancy frame or anything (unless you want to). During the tournament, take a few shots throughout the day and then you can get them printed. Insert the photos in a thank you card and send them to your client. Once you're certain the photos have arrived at your client's office, follow up with a phone call and schedule a follow-up lunch or coffee meeting to discuss future work.

Industry Events and Conferences

There are hundreds of professional organizations and conferences held each year across the country. These events are great ways to connect with potential clients and other professionals who can refer you to potential clients. Depending on your industry, you're probably already aware of different events you might want to attend. In the architectural, engineering, and construction industry, popular organizations include the Urban Land Institute (ULI), Associated Builders and Contracts (ABC), and the American Institute of Architects (AIA). Many of these organizations have monthly luncheons that feature pertinent educational topics for the industry.

Sponsor

Sponsoring an educational event or monthly event is a great way to raise visibility for your firm. Sponsoring one time may have some impact but it won't move mountains. Once you target specific events that are target-rich environments for your prospective clients, make it part of your plan to sponsor several events throughout the year. Also, if you're sponsoring an event, sometimes your firm will have the opportunity to do a three- to five-minute commercial advertising your firm. If you have the opportunity, practice ahead of time so that you advertise your firm in the most positive light.

Participation on a Panel

A great way to raise visibility for your firm is to get speaking opportunities at industry events. If you are the marketing or business development professional, you may not be the best person to speak at an event, you may instead want to work on securing a speaking opportunity for one of your principals or senior staff members. To get one of your firm's senior staff members on a panel, you will need to find out who is organizing an upcoming event on a specific topic. A good way to make sure one of your firm's staff members gets on a panel is to participate in the planning committee for a given topic. Your participation on the planning committee may not be a guarantee for getting a speaking opportunity for one of the key members of your firm, but it helps to stack the odds in your favor. Also, if you're part of the planning committee, you may also have the opportunity to get to know some of the speakers for various panels and that can be quite beneficial if they are also prospective clients for your firm.

Promoting Your Clients
Another reason to participate in educational panels and professional events is it may elevate your standing in the eyes of a prospective client. If you participate in organizations or are board members of organizations that a majority of your clients participate in, they will start to recognize your brand and in most cases, appreciate that your firm has similar interests as them. Participating in these types of organizations gives you an opportunity to meet up with prospective clients and help them to see you as a partner already. Once they get to know you in this setting and how you work, it will make the transition to a business relationship a little easier.

As you can see, there are many ways you can engage and work with prospective clients before you ask for their business. Participating in industry events and conferences will lay the groundwork towards successful working relationships with prospective clients.

Press and Media Coverage
Getting the word out about the innovative practices your firm engages in can be a huge challenge depending on how niche your industry is. Conversely, knowing how to handle a crisis is important to managing the overall reputation of your firm. I really only have one recommendation for managing press and media coverage for your firm: hire a professional PR consultant. When it comes to managing your overall reputation, crisis management, and strategic communications, the right PR consultant can focus on your firm's reputation while you focus on winning more work and promoting your firm in other valuable ways. Typically, most PR firms work on retainer, and depending on the services you are looking for, the price range can vary quite a bit. If you really want to see your company's online and industry profile rise, you may want to consider hiring a professional PR firm to help you. In this section, I've listed several ways your PR consultant will help your firm.

Crisis Communications
Crisis management and crisis communication is a must-have in your plan. Crisis management may seem like something that may never be important for your firm, and I hope you never have to weather a storm, however, a professional with resources in place to handle any crisis can be a lifesaver for your company. Perhaps one of the most important crisis management services a PR firm can offer is media training. Knowing how

to respond to media inquiries in both positive and negative situations is critical to managing the overall reputation for your firm. PR consultants may not be cheap, but I assure you they can be worth their weight in gold during a crisis. In this day and age, with how quickly information can spread, make sure you have the best professional resources in place to manage your reputation.

Established Media Relationships

PR firms work with the media daily. In some cases, your PR consultant or your PR firm's staff may have worked for a newspaper or news station. Your PR consultant's relationships make a huge difference when it comes to pushing out great content as well as making sure the right information gets out quickly. Sure, there are some great online resources where you can go and place your press release for a small fee, however, when you hire a PR firm, you're hiring a known entity to represent your brand. A good analogy might be how you respond to a company like FedEx showing up to deliver a package you're not expecting versus some guy named Joe Smith. Chances are, you'll be a little more comfortable accepting a package from FedEx and reporters are a little more willing to accept a story pitched by your PR consultant than you personally.

Online Presence

Many PR firms now offer consulting services to help your firm manage blogging and social media, which is a great option if it's within your budget. "But wait!", you might be thinking, "I'm a digital native and I've been on social media since I could crawl." Great! But if you're working for a professional services firm, the most critical component of your job is to make sure you help your firm win work through marketing and business development efforts. If you spend most of your time working on proposals and business development, you want to outsource what you can. If you can outsource social media and blogging to ensure that it gets done regularly, it will give you the time you need to focus on winning new business. I have seen plenty of firms rebrand their website and start a social media campaign to capitalize on rebranding, but as time goes on, these efforts fizzle out. If your firm can hire a PR or marketing firm to help you manage your digital marketing efforts, you should do it.

Managing your PR Consultant

As you can see, hiring the right PR consultant can help you manage your firm's community and online reputations. Before you hire a PR consultant, make sure you discuss weekly and monthly deliverables so you can stay on top of how they're helping your firm succeed in managing its reputation. Ask for regular updates and ensure that your key messages are being shared and your goals are being met.

Raising Your Firm's Profile Through Writing Opportunities

Creating ways for your professionals to become well known in their respective industries is critical to success in service-based businesses. One of the best resources I've seen for giving professionals a clear path to success in their respective field is Kevin Harrington and Daniel Priestley's book, "Key Person of Influence. The Five-Step Method to Become One of the Most Highly Valued and Highly Paid People in Your Industry." A critical step to becoming a "key person of influence" is getting published. In this section, I'll elaborate more on what types of writing opportunities you can find for your key staff to help solidify their status as respected leaders in their industry.

LinkedIn Blogging

At the bare minimum, members of your senior staff should create a blog on LinkedIn and begin writing about key issues that fall under their realm of expertise. Usually, it's the marketing person who ghost-writes these articles and then asks the senior staff member to post the article on LinkedIn. And in some cases, the marketing professional even posts it for the senior staff member. The bottom line is, make sure that articles are getting written on a regular basis -- 300-500 words is plenty. If writing 300-500 words seems intimidating right off the bat, help senior staff members post on well-known blogs. If this even seems like too much work for you and your staff, you can hire a digital marketing firm to help you. Once your staff has digital content online, you can then share links to this content via your social media channels.

Trade Publications

Every industry has trade publications. Contact editors for your industry's trade publications to look for writing opportunities. Every large trade publication has an editorial calendar. You can do a little internet research and find out which journals are publishing articles on certain types of subjects well in advance. When I find a trade publication focusing on an area that I know is a specialty of one of my team members, I reach out to the editor by email and let them know that I have the perfect person to write the article for them. It may take a couple of phone calls and a couple of emails to get a response, but it's worth it when you do. Just remember that magazines are working several months ahead – if you want to offer an article for the June issue, you should reach out to the editor by March at the latest. Smaller publications may not have an editorial calendar fully fleshed out. You may want to start with these organizations first, and once you're published in one of these, it will be easier to get published in a larger publication. A PR consultant can make this process even easier and can help you identify which publications would be best for your firm and also reach out to the editors.

What's Involved with Writing an Article

Once you sell an editor on your expertise and ability to write an article for them, now it's time to do it. Usually, you'll receive clear instructions on the subject matter and length. Most publications have a style guide to follow. In most of the firms I've worked in, a senior staff member has yet to write their own article. Usually it's an 80/20 approach. I draft most of the article after interviewing them extensively and then they proofread and make changes as they see fit. Do not plan on a key staff member at your firm writing most of the article by him or herself. You will miss the deadline. In addition, while you will be able to mention your firm's name and offer quotes from your experts, most publications will ask that the article be informational rather than promotional, so keep that in mind while drafting content.

Make sure you have the time, resources, and support to assist in producing the article. Many PR firms can help you with this part of the process as well. But depending on your budget, you may have to do some of the heavy lifting of writing the article by yourself.

Making the Most of Getting Published

Once the article is published, make sure you get the most out of it! Write a blog on your website and post a link to the article if it's in a digital form as well. Make sure your senior staff members post it on their LinkedIn page (updates their profile to add it their list of publications), share it on your LinkedIn page, your company's LinkedIn page, and see if you can get some of your other staff members to share the article as well. You can get even more use out of the article by thinking of different lead-ins to the article and posting it on Twitter a few times a day for the next week. It also doesn't hurt to post a link to the article on your Facebook page as well. When it comes to sharing the article, the more, the merrier! Encourage your friends and family to share the good news as well.

SUMMARY

In this chapter, we focused on ways you can increase positive perception of your firm's brand. You learned how to:
- Make the most out of your tradeshows and connect with as many prospective clients as possible;
- Build on your client relationships through tournaments and events;
- Work with press and get media coverage for your firm; and
- Raise your company's profile through writing opportunities.

After reading this book, you now have everything you need to make your first year in marketing professional services a huge success.

REFERENCES

Chapter 2
Harrington, Kevin, and Daniel Priestley. Key Person of Influence: The Five-Step Method to Become One of the Most Highly Valued and Highly Paid People in Your Industry. Gorleston, England: Rethink Press, 2015.

Chapter 3
Bolton, Holly R., Julie Huval, David M. Shelton, and Ron Worth. A/E/C Marketing Fundamentals: Your Keys to Success. Ed. Richard A. Belle. Alexandria: SMPS Publications, 2015. Digital.

"SWOT Analysis: Discover New Opportunities, Manage and Eliminate Threats." (Strengths, Weaknesses Opportunities, Threats). Accessed December 03 2016, https://www.mindtools.com/pages/article/newTMC_05.htm.

Chapter 4
Post, Peggy, Peter Post, and Emily Post. Emily Post's The Etiquette Advantage in Business: Personal Skills for Professional Success. New York: HarperResource, 2005.

Chapter 6
Sant, Tom. Persuasive Business Proposals: Writing to Win More Customers, Clients, and Contracts. New York: AMACOM, 2004.

Chapter 7
2016, Lee Frederiksen Ph.D. | October 3. "Find Your Differentiator: 21 Ways to Gain a Competitive Advantage for Your Firm | Hinge Marketing." Hinge Marketing. October 03, 2016. Accessed December 08, 2016.https://hingemarketing.com/blog/story/find-your-differentiator-21-ways-to-gain-a-competitive-advantage-for-your-f

Chapter 8
Cobb, Neil, and Charlie Divine. Writing Business Bids & Proposals for Dummies. Chichester, West Sussex: John Wiley & Sons, 2016.

"What Are Proposal Themes and Why Are They Important?" What Are Proposal Themes and Why Are They Important? N.p., n.d. Web. 05 Jan. 2017.

Chapter 9
Cobb, Neil, and Charlie Divine. Writing Business Bids & Proposals for Dummies. Chichester, West Sussex: John Wiley & Sons, 2016.

Chapter 10

Asher, Joey. How to Win a Pitch: The Five Fundamentals That Will Distinguish You from the Competition. Atlanta, GA: Persuasive Speaker Press, 2009.

Reynolds, Garr. Presentation Zen: Simple Ideas on Presentation Design and Delivery. Berkeley, CA: New Riders Pub., 2008. 85-89.

Chapter 11

"CAN-SPAM Act and How It Effects Your Campaigns." CTCTSupport. Accessed December 05, 2016. http://knowledgebase.constantcontact.com/

Chapter 12

Gannon, Drew. "8 Tricks of the Trade Show." Inc.com. May 13, 2011. Accessed December 05, 2016. https://www.inc.com/ss/8-tricks-trade-show

Harrington, Kevin, and Daniel Priestley. Key Person of Influence: The Five-Step Method to Become One of the Most Highly Valued and Highly Paid People in Your Industry. Gorleston, England: Rethink Press, 2015.

Hoff, Lew. "TSNN Trade Show News." Tricks of the Trade Show: Engagement | TSNN Trade Show News. Accessed December 05, 2016. http://www.tsnn.com/news-blogs/tricks-trade-show-engagement.

ABOUT THE AUTHOR

Chaz Ross-Munro has been a professional services marketer for more than 10 years and has helped secure more than $600 million in contracts in both the public and private sectors.

Ross-Munro began her career at the St. Louis, Missouri location of Burns & McDonnell, an engineering and architecture firm based in Kansas City, Missouri. While struggling with her first RFP response at Burns & McDonnell, Ross-Munro was introduced to the Society of Marketing Professional Services (SMPS) on the recommendation of one of her coworkers in business development. SMPS proved to be crucial to Ross-Munro's development and she has since obtained the Certified Professional Services Marketer (CPSM) designation and most recently served as the SMPS Tampa Bay President 2015-2016.

Ross-Munro later joined the Atlanta office of Bovis Lend Lease (now Lend Lease), an ENR globally-ranked general contractor based in Australia. While at Lend Lease, Ross-Munro learned how large companies leverage national marketing resources to produce successful sales strategies and high-impact proposals. Building on what she learned in the Atlanta office, Ross-Munro transferred to the company's new Tampa office. Since the Tampa location for Bovis Lend Lease was essentially a start-up, Ross-Munro was responsible for creating the marketing presence for this new office. Within two years, the Tampa office secured more than $300 million in new contracts and Ross-Munro's responsibilities expanded to focus on the southeast region, which included managing marketing responsibilities for Charlotte, Raleigh, Washington D.C., Atlanta, and Miami.

In 2013, Ross-Munro received her Master of Science in Entrepreneurship in Applied Technologies from the University of South Florida. While in the Entrepreneurship program, Ross-Munro gained a deeper understanding of business planning, sources of funding, mergers/acquisitions, and strategic marketing approaches for new products and services. She now infuses her entrepreneurial passion into her daily activities to build opportunities for clients selling professional services.

CPSIA information can be obtained
at www.ICGtesting.com
Printed in the USA
LVOW05s1138190218
566962LV00001B/1/P